# THE ASBESTOS WIVES

## Kay McElhinney

## B & K Publishers

*The Asbestos Wives*

This is a work of fiction, based in part, upon the personal experience of the author, a former Colorado District Court Clerk. This Court handled all of the asbestos litigation filed in its jurisdiction.

Fourth Printing-February 2020

Published by B & K Publishers
Woodland Park, Colorado

ISBN: 978-0-9986020--8-0 (soft cover)
Library of Congress Control Number 2019913775

Published in the United States of America *https://bkfreelance-writersandpublishers.com/*

# Dedication

"*The Asbestos Wives*" is dedicated to the thousands of men, women and children who have become ill from their exposure to asbestos and to all of them who died from asbestosis and mesothelioma.

# *Preface*

Asbestos has been around a long time. It was first identified in prehistoric times. It occurs naturally in large deposits on every continent in the world. Archeologists uncovered asbestos fibers in debris dating back some 750,000 years to the Stone Age. As early as 4000 BC, asbestos fibers apparently were used for lamp wicks and candles. When asbestos underwent scientific-geological scrutiny, its heat resistant properties were confirmed with some enthusiasm for industrial and manufacturing applications. Its negative effects on people were documented by the Greeks and Romans among them, Greek geographer Strabo who noted a sickness of the lungs in slaves who wove asbestos into cloth. [1]

The life altering effects of asbestos include permanent disability and more often than not, death. The illnesses and deaths from the effects of asbestos have been the subject of civil litigation in the United States for at least the past forty years. This litigation is very complex to prepare and costly to take to trial. The asbestos lawyers and their support staffs treat each case very seriously and often sustain emotional fall-out resulting from their association with, and representation of, these seriously injured clients.

The first asbestos litigators were pioneers of sorts. They took cases of injured workers and their fam-

4

ilies on a contingent fee basis. They did not earn attorney's fees unless they prevailed against the manufacturers and distributors either through settlements or court verdicts. They also invested very large sums of their own capital preparing these cases with no reimbursement unless they prevailed for their clients. The economic risks were great and the rewards were even greater.

Asbestos litigators are known in the legal profession as product liability attorneys. They became experts on the product called asbestos and cast a wide net throughout the country reeling in injured workers from many of the trades including mine workers, plumbers, ship builders, auto mechanics, insulation installers, and demolition contractors. When they were successful for their clients against the corporate giants such as Johns Mansville and W.R. Grace, their pay days were huge, often in the millions of dollars.

As these attorneys began to prevail in their efforts, their firm bank accounts grew as did their personal accounts. Soon many of these lawyers became millionaires with more money for their personal use than they ever imagined. With their new monetary status in life some developed an inflated attitude toward others, especially women. They realized that many, young, attractive females, some of whom were associate attorneys and paralegals, were available and attracted to them. They made it known they represented people injured by the deadly effects of asbestos and that they had acquired large bank accounts as a result of their humanitarian efforts.

Young ladies were attracted to these attorneys because of their wealth and status in the legal community. They made themselves available for the "catch" not realizing the consequences that came with the "release."

Most of the asbestos lawyers were married. Their trial work took them from their home turf to other states. They often took their wives along for the trip and a mini vacation. These wives became acquainted and ultimately good friends. They shopped together, lunched together, and as one would expect, they also drank together. As the liquor took effect, they began to share their most personal thoughts, frustrations, and anxieties about husbands, family and married life. Thus, came into being what was called "The Asbestos Wives."

This book is a fictional representation of some of these attorneys and their wives; the demise of their marriages, the resulting marital settlements, and the good the wives accomplished with their new-found wealth.

## 1

# Victoria Alexis Murphy

Her husband was one of the top attorneys in the country. He was handsome and very wealthy. They lived a life of leisure. It was every girl's dream. However, was the extreme wealth worth the sacrifice?

Her name was Victoria, her friends called her Vicki. She was born to middle class parents and raised in a small town in Colorado. She had a younger sister named Anna.

When Vicki was seventeen and Anna was fifteen, their father died quite suddenly. With his death, they lost any protection they had from their abusive, vindictive mother, Irene.

Anna asked Vicki, "Now what will we do; you will go away soon, and I will be left alone with our mother."

Vicki answered, "I will protect you and when I leave, you will go with me."

Vicki knew protecting Anna from their mother was going to be very difficult since she felt totally vulnerable herself. She tried to understand her mother and wanted her to be more like her friends' mothers who took care of their children, encouraging them to be the best they could, instead of berating them.

Irene was born right before the Great Depression and it had a profound effect on her entire life. She didn't like being poor and her ultimate goal in life was to be a millionaire. She married at eighteen, had Vicki at nineteen, Anna at twenty-one, and was widowed at thirty-six. From then on, she set out to make money, dominate men and her children.

Vicki's childhood was lonely and she lived in constant fear of her mother, who was physically, verbally and emotionally abusive. If Vicki did well in school, it wasn't good enough, and if she excelled at sports, it wasn't good enough. Irene berated Vicki every chance she could.

"I know you will get pregnant and when you do, I'm not taking care of it." Irene informed Vicki when she was twelve.

When Vicki told her mom that Jack and she were engaged, Irene said, "Sleep with Jack if you must, just don't marry him."

"You will never see me alive again." Irene told Vicki as she was waiting to walk down the aisle to marry Jack.

Anna didn't fare any better.

"You will grow up to be just as worthless as your sister!" Irene would yell at Anna.

"I'm not taking you in with your bastard child, either." Irene would scream at Anna when she was interested in a boy.

The physical beatings were almost more than Vicki could stand. The last one was when she was eighteen. Due to this abuse, Vicki felt insecure and lacked a sense of self-worth. These feelings would mold the rest of her life and have a direct effect on the decisions she made.

She felt helpless when she heard Anna screaming as their mother beat her. Irene would lock Vicki in the room she Anna shared. Vicki would lay on her bed and cry for Anna.

Vicki prayed, please God make it stop; what did we do to deserve this?

Returning to the room in tears, Anna asked Vicki,

"What are we going to do? She's going to kill us."

"I don't know Anna, we have to get out of here, I'm not sure how, but we will," cried Vicki.

After their father died, Irene took up with men who were rough around the edges and they abused Vicki and Anna physically and emotionally. To get away from the abuse, Vicki and Anna moved in with their grandparents, Bill and Connie who truly loved them.

Bill and Connie had a younger daughter named Donna who was killed in an automobile accident a week before her fifteenth birthday. Neither Bill nor Connie totally recovered from the loss: having their two granddaughters with them helped ease the pain.

Shortly after the girls moved into their grandparents' house, Irene moved to a small, isolated mountain town with one of her boyfriends. Vicki and Anna seldom saw their mother.

Irene didn't send any money to help with the girls' support. This put a heavy burden on their grandparents who gladly made any sacrifice necessary.

Sports were Vicki's escape from her tortured life. She

played soccer and was captain of her team in high school. She went to college on a soccer scholarship. The recognition was good for her and the physical exertion helped her forget about her mother.

Anna's outlet was painting. She spent hours looking at the sky, or watching a bird, then painting it perfectly from memory. Her art teacher praised her talent and the pride was visible in her eyes after such accolades.

Vicki was tall, athletic, with long dark hair, and big brown eyes. She had a warm smile and people were drawn to her. She was half Italian with beautiful olive skin that was always tan in the summer. Because of soccer, she was trim and fit and could wear clothes with ease. She had been told she should be a model, however, Vicki had higher goals.

Anna was the opposite of Vicki. She was petite with light blonde hair and blue eyes. Their father had blue eyes and Vicki often wondered if she and Anna had the same father. Anna was fair and didn't like the sun. Since she was petite, she had trouble finding clothes to fit her small frame.

"Vicki, you always look great in anything you're wearing. I wish I were tall like you." Anna said softly.

"Anna, I have always wanted to be petite and blonde with blue eyes; maybe God mixed us up." Vicki said with a laugh.

Vicki was popular with older boys in high school. She dated fellow students, as well as those from nearby high schools and colleges. Even though she dated extensively, she felt an emptiness and an unfulfilled longing for love and acceptance.

Vicki became close friends with one of her fellow students, Jack, and was welcomed into his family as one of their own. She had her own bedroom in their home and often stayed there. They even welcomed Anna into their home and had a spare room where she would sleep. For the first time in their lives, Vicki and Anna felt they were part of a loving family.

Vicki's favorite time of year with Jack's family was Christmas. Sarah, Jack's mom, and Vicki would start cooking for the season months before, freezing cookies, cakes and other special goodies. Even though Vicki was part Italian, Sarah had to teach her how to cook Italian food.

Vicki's mother hadn't taught her any skills for managing her own home.

"Vicki, you are a wonderful cook and Jack is so happy when you are around." Sarah told Vicki. "You are so good to Anna and we love having her here, too."

"Thank you, Sarah, you are the mother I wish I had." Vicki lamented.

"Vicki, your mom loves you in her own way. When you are a mom, you will understand her."

"I made a decision long ago that I would never have children because I'm afraid I would be a mom like mine." Vicki confessed.

"Oh no, dear, if you and Jack marry someday, you will have to have children because he is Catholic."

"We'll see," said Vicki.

Vicki and Anna loved staying with Jack's family during the holidays. Their Italian traditions ensured a lively and fun-filled time, punctuated with large meals with all their favorite food. Christmas Eve was a wonderful time, not ending until three or four Christmas morning.

There was much food, wine and loud celebrating after midnight mass. Bill and Connie would arrive early Christmas morning to share in the joy and happiness of the day, although with heavy hearts because of Irene, but they hid their feelings well.

Vicki was always interested in the law and clerked for an attorney during high school summer breaks and part time during college. She was responsible for her own spending money and extras while in college since her scholarship only paid for tuition and books. She didn't want to burden her grandparents with these additional expenses.

After graduating from high school, Anna went to Chicago to study art at the Chicago Art Institute. She was successful in her studies and happy in a relation"ship with Sam, one of her professors.

"Oh Vicki, Sam is wonderful to me. I didn't know men could be so kind and gentle, except for dad." Anna bubbled.

Vicki was truly happy for her sister and told her so.

With a sigh, she wondered if she would ever find true love. Jack wasn't the one.

Vicki and Jack were carrying on a long-distance relationship. Jack attended a well-known Catholic university and was lonely and unhappy. Their senior year, Jack proposed to Vicki and she accepted; *a voice inside told her not to do it.* Vicki didn't feel the happiness that Anna talked about.

Jack and Vicki were married the September following their graduation from college. As Vicki was walking down the aisle, she realized she was marrying the idea of his family and not out of love for Jack. She also realized she was marrying him to get away from her mother.

Irene came to the wedding and told everyone she had paid for the entire wedding, which was far from the truth. Vicki and Jack had saved as much money as they could and his parents paid the balance. Irene's contribution was one-hundred dollars and a book of green stamps. Vicki was embarrassed when Irene started an argument with Vicki's aunts and uncles in the parking lot about why they had come to the wedding.

"You are only here to see if you can get some of my money since your brother died!" Irene screamed.

"We came because we love Vicki and want to see her happy." Uncle Cecil replied calmly.

Bill and Connie finally had to calm Irene down and take her to their house where she continued to rant and rave about the wedding.

Anna, Vicki's only attendant, put her arms around Vicki and comforted her.

"You are free now," she whispered.

Vicki replied, "I sure hope so. I love you and I'm so glad you are happy."

"I have a secret; Sam and I eloped and I am pregnant, however, I don't want mom to ever know." smiled Anna.

"Your secret is safe with me. Wow, I'm going to be an aunt!" beamed Vicki. "This is the best day ever."

Jack decided to attend graduate school, which meant Vicki's dream of attending law school was put on hold. She felt it was more important for Jack to fulfill his dreams than to think about her own. Vicki worked while Jack pursued his Master's Degree. After receiving his M.A., Jack decided he wanted to go to law school.

Vicki was working for a large public law firm, specializing in criminal law and Jack hoped he could get a job there after he graduated. Vicki decided she had enough of supporting Jack, who was turning into a career student.

"What next, medical school? What about my dream of law school? You never mentioned you were interested in the law." cried Vicki.

"Sweetie, I'm doing it for us."

"BS" screamed Vicki and she fled out the front door.

She called Anna and could hear the happiness in Anna's voice. Anna had given birth to a little girl and named her Bonnie.

"Leave him Vicki, you have so much going for you and you deserve to be happy."

"I don't know, I don't have the energy to leave him right now. What would I do?" asked Vicki, although she didn't want an answer.

Finally, after Jack's first year of law school, he decided he would volunteer at the public law firm where Vicki worked. She had had enough and left Jack.

After the end of her marriage to Jack, Vicki moved to Stone Mountain, Montana and found a job in the court system working for Judge Robert Gresham, in the civil trial division.

Asbestos litigation was in its infant stages and the cases were very complex. Due to the complexities, all of these cases were assigned to one judge to hear all motions, settlement negotiations and trials, if the cases didn't settle.

Judge Gresham was the judge to whom all the asbestos cases were assigned.

Judge Gresham said, "Vicki, since these cases take so

much time, I will depend on you to keep the court running smoothly. I won't have time to schedule all the appearances the attorneys request. I will trust you to determine if they are really necessary, find an opening on the docket and coordinate with all attorneys. There could be twenty or more attorneys on the docket at one time. I will need you in the courtroom with me to schedule hearings. Do you think you are up to it?"

"Of course, your Honor, it sounds exciting."

"When we are not in court or have attorneys in chambers, call me Bob."

Vicki was very glad to find a job so soon after moving. Now, she had to find a place to live and move out of the motel she was staying in.

On the edge of town was a large property with a house and cottage. A quiet stream flowed through the property. Vicki had seen the property while driving around to acquaint herself with Stone Mountain. She went to the house and knocked on the front door. An elderly, distinguished man came to the door.

"Hello, my name is Vicki Murphy. I have just moved to Stone Mountain and I'm looking for a place to live. I will be working for Judge Gresham. By chance, is your cottage available?"

"Hello, Vicki Murphy. My name is George Martin. My wife, Kathleen, is at the cottage right now making a list of repairs and upgrades. Let's go look at it."

On their way to the cottage, George explained that he and Bob Gresham were good friends and if Bob hired her, he was sure Vicki would be a good tenant.

As soon as she stepped through the front door, Vicki fell in love with the cottage. There was a large living room with a stone fireplace and a deck that looked over the valley and river. There were two quite small, very nice bedrooms. Each bedroom had its own bathroom, ideal for Anna, Sam and Bonnie's visits. One bedroom even had an alcove for baby-Bonnie's crib.  The kitchen was just adequate.

"Kathleen, honey, this is Vicki and she's looking for a place to live. She's working for Bob Gresham."

"Hello Mrs. Martin. I love the cottage, and I would like to get a dog to keep me company. Do you allow pets?"

"Hello my dear, please call me Kathleen. I am making a list of repairs and upgrades to the kitchen. We did the bathrooms last year. We would love to have you live here and yes; you may have a dog."

"Oh, thank you so much. This is a great day. I have a job and a home! Now, we have to discuss rent and deposits."

After they agreed on the rent and the other terms, Vicki was floating on air. Since it was still early in the day, she decided to go to the humane society and 'just look'.

Sitting in a cage was the most beautiful husky Vicki had ever seen. She was grey, black and white with amazing blue eyes. As Vicki walked up to the cage, the husky greeted her with a low howl and wagging tail. Vicki was in love.

After talking to the attendant and agreeing that the dog was hers, Vicki called Mrs. Martin and asked if she could move in now? She said the contractors could work on the kitchen while she was at work.

"Of course, we can even watch your dog while you are at work." Kathleen offered.

Vicki had a job, a home and a dog. She named the dog Juno. When she called out 'Juno,' the dog wagged its tail, and gave a loud, happy howl.

She called Anna that night and for the first time in a long time, Vicki was excited and happy.

Vicki started her job a week later. She settled into her new home with Juno who loved chasing the critters that showed up on the property.

However, Vicki wouldn't let Juno chase the deer and kept her in at night because of the night visitors, including bears.

Vicki went to work at the court and she was thrown into the middle of the asbestos litigation. She felt right at home from the first day. She met several of the other court clerks and one in particular, a lady named Barbara, seemed like a good match for her. Barbara worked for another trial judge and they had much in common. They became close friends from day one.

Vicki also became friends with many of the attorneys who appeared regularly before Judge Gresham.

Often, one attorney Ted Winter, needed to schedule appearances before the court. To do so, he had to work closely with Vicki since she scheduled all court matters.

It was well known that Vicki was single. What wasn't so well known was that she was not looking for a committed relationship. She was finally finding out who she was and enjoying being single. She dated often. Also, she enjoyed being home with Juno.

Juno would look at Vicki with her blue eyes and it seemed the dog knew exactly what Vicki was feeling. When Vicki cried, Juno was at her side and would comfort her with soft howling and husky talk.

One weekend when Vicki and Barb were sitting on

Vicki's deck drinking a glass of wine, she asked Barb about Ted Winter.

"Why, are you interested in him?"

"Not really, although he seems to always need something from the court that we could handle over the phone."

"Well, he is quite the man about town. From what I hear, he was very successful in high school, college and law school. He went Ivy League for college and law school. He has an absolutely amazing cabin on the island in the lake. I've never been there but you hear things. He was married to his high school sweetheart and it didn't last. I heard that he was unfaithful many times."

"Hum sounds like the type of guy I wouldn't want to date. He would never be interested in someone like me." replied Vicki.

Vicki's life was good. Would this be her life forever?

# 2

## Theodore Justin Winter

He was "the man" about town. Tall and muscular, with a shock of dark hair reminiscent of movie stars of old; his piercing blue eyes revealed his moods and feelings. Born into a life of wealth and privilege, he was a member of the 'lucky sperm club'. His name was Theodore Justin Winter; he preferred just plain Ted.

His athletic prowess was well known in the local schools as were his propensities to dazzle the ladies. He was charming, well dressed and soft spoken; underneath this all-American exterior was a bubbling caldron of testosterone. He had been the big man on campus in high school and college. In high school, he maintained a 4.0 grade-point average and lettered in football and baseball.

His parents worked hard to instill the work ethic in both their children. So, during his high school years, he and a friend, Ben, lived in Libby, Montana and worked in the vermiculite (commonly called zonolite) mines that produced large amounts of asbestos dust.

So, from ages sixteen to eighteen, when he graduated

19

from high school, he was exposed to asbestos dust for three months at a time.

He played football at Harvard, graduated summa cum laude and immediately applied to Yale where he earned an MBA. After receiving his MBA, he attended law school at Harvard where he was a member of law review and graduated first in his class. With this distinguished education, he could practice law wherever he wanted. He was offered jobs with many of the most prestigious law firms in the country.

Ted loved Montana and wanted to go home, so he accepted a job with the Stone Mountain law firm of Keller, Lewis and Schuler. He started as a law clerk while studying for the Montana Bar Exam. He passed the Bar Exam on his first try, and was ready to take on the world representing the oppressed and injured.

He was well liked and admired by members of the local bar and bench. Within three years he was made a full partner and settled into his life of law, outdoor activities and an extremely active social life.

Fun to be with, he was always among invited guests at most social events in the Stone Mountain area.

Stone Mountain was a haven for the wealthy. Many retired CEO's, doctors, lawyers and trust-fund babies lived there. The standard of living was very high. It was located in a beautiful valley in northern Montana, surrounded by high mountains boasting lush streams, native trees and vegetation, that were ablaze with many colors in the fall. There was a very large lake in the valley, Lake Stone. Ted built his home on an island in the lake.

He purchased the island when he was still in college, knowing someday he would return and build his dream log cabin there. The "cabin" was over six-thousand square feet and had every modern convenience. The setting was spectacular.

To get to the cabin, he used a restored Chris Craft that he kept in a marina on the mainland. In winter, he drove his Range Rover over the frozen lake.

He had an inflated opinion of himself; some said he was an egomaniac. He hadn't yet suffered the loss of a family member or friend. His main fault was his arrogance and lack of empathy for people.

Life was extremely easy for him.

He had been married to Ann, his high school sweetheart. He didn't remain faithful to her and the marriage ended. He immediately started enjoying the life of the bachelor about town. Ann, on the other hand, had to endure hearing about who he was dating and all about his social life.

She thought about leaving Stone Mountain, however she couldn't stand the thought of being away from Ted. In tears, one night she called him and begged him to come back to her.

"Ted, I can't take this anymore. Please, please let's try again. I will do anything to get you back."

"Ann, you know it won't work and quite frankly, I'm so much happier without you tying me down and always accusing me of being unfaithful. You knew what I was like when we got married. You knew I wouldn't change and you knew I needed to have many women to keep me happy." said Ted, smiling to himself.

He was dating many women, usually several at a time. His best friend, Ben, told him that he had a definite need to sample all the cookies in the cookie jar.

One of Ted's hobbies was fly fishing, almost always catch and release. His attitude toward women was very similar, catching them, taking them into his bed, releasing them, and moving on to the next one.

He had no plans to marry again, since he was enjoying his bachelorhood far too much.

He was assigned to represent the plaintiffs in the firm's asbestos litigation. The firm was the premier firm representing people who had been afflicted with asbestosis or mesothelioma. The clients were mostly blue-collar workers, including many who had been in the military, others who were construction workers or mechanics, and all had come into contact with asbestos.

Taking on this challenge, Ted soon developed the reputation of being one of the best products liability attorneys in the country in the area of asbestos litigation. There always seemed to be a bulge in the trousers of his box-like-fitting Brooks Brother's suits.

The bulge got noticeably larger whenever he appeared at Vicki's desk.

Obviously, and almost uncontrollably taken with Vicki, Ted pursued her like he was fly fishing for the most beautiful rainbow trout in the Henry's Fork River.

He appeared at her desk daily.

"Hey Vicki, you're looking especially nice today." he would say to start the conversation. "I bet your boyfriend really likes having you on his arm."

"Hi Ted, thank you for the compliment. I don't want a boyfriend, so just knock it off."

The challenge was presented, and Ted was not one to back down from a challenge, especially when it involved a woman, he was interested in. Finally, after six weeks, Ted asked Vicki out on a date.

"Vicki, would you like to go hiking with me next Saturday in Water Canyon? It's beautiful there and you can see the whole valley from the top."

Playing hard to get, Vicki replied, "No thank you Ted, I have plans on Saturday."

Ted left. He was not discouraged, knowing that his persistence would eventually win him a date with her.

After work that day, Vicki met Barb and some other court clerks for a glass of wine at The Verdict, a local establishment where most of the legal community met for drinks and dinner.

"You will never guess who asked me out." Vicki said.

"Who?" asked Barb.

"Ted Winter. He's way out of my league and I don't think I can handle his personality. He wants me to go hiking with him and I'm not sure I should?"

"You're kidding me!" shrieked Barb. "He's the best catch in Stone Mountain, in fact, in the whole State of Montana." A week later, Ted tried again. And again, Vicki declined.

Barb told Vicki, "Go out with him, just GO and have a good time. It's not like you're going to marry him; besides, he drives a Porsche."

"Maybe you have a point. He is good looking and I know he's not looking for a permanent relationship. I wonder what my Judge would say, because Ted handles all the asbestos cases for his firm?"

"Your Judge doesn't need to know."

So, when Ted tried again, Vicki accepted. The date and time were set. Ted was going to pick her up at her cottage and they were going hiking in Water Canyon.

On the appointed day, Vicki was thinking about the upcoming date when her doorbell rang. Standing there, three hours early, was Ted Winter. He walked into the room, taking most of the oxygen around him as he entered.

No one should be that self-confident and controlled, Vicki thought.

"Hi Vicki, I was in the neighborhood and thought we might as well go early." he said without any regard for what Vicki was doing.

"Well, I was in the middle of something; I guess I can change so we can go now." Vicki said, more than a little irritated.

Vicki changed into hiking clothes and they were off in the Porsche with the top down.

When Vicki returned home, she called Barb and told her about Ted showing up early and that it was just an 'okay' date.

"I have no particular feelings one way or the other for him." Vicki reported to Barb. "He was self-assured, fun to be with, and didn't talk about himself but, I wasn't particularly attracted to him."

"Will you go out with him again, if he asks?"

"Hum, don't know for sure. If we do start going out, I think I should tell Judge Gresham about it because it could cause conflicts in the asbestos cases. I'm not going to worry about that until he calls again."

The following work day, Ted was at Vicki's desk.

"Hi Gorgeous, want to go to lunch?"

As they were walking out of her office, Vicki saw Judge Gresham watching them.

She enjoyed the lunch and thought it might be fun to see Ted more often.

When she got back to work, she asked if she could talk to Judge Gresham privately. In his office, she told him that she had dated Ted.

"Bob, I want you to know that I have seen Ted Winter a couple of times. I think he will ask me out again."

"Well, I don't see a problem at this point. You realize you shouldn't talk about the asbestos cases with him. Has he asked you anything about them?" inquired the Judge, sounding concerned.

"No, he hasn't mentioned anything about work and, if he does ask, I will tell him I can't talk about the asbestos cases."

"Vicki, I feel I should tell you something else. When I first started practicing law, I represented the Winter family.

Ted was usually my client because of small types of trouble he would get into. I have total respect for his parents; however, Ted is trouble and I would hate to see you get hurt. He really doesn't respect women, so please be careful."

After the talk with the Judge, *a small voice in Vicki's head asked, of all people, why do you think he is interested in you?*

She quickly put the *voice* out of her mind.

That weekend, Ted and Vicki spent Saturday together shopping for dinner and then crossed the lake in his Chris Craft to the cabin. Vicki walked in the front door and the house took her breath away. Although it was evident from the furnishings and décor a male lived there, it was beautifully done and she immediately had a thought of living there. Shaking her head, she put that thought out of her mind.

"Well, what do you think?"

"Absolutely beautiful Ted. You must love living here. Look at the view."

They went into the large kitchen and started preparing their dinner of shrimp scampi, salad, white wine and homemade cookies Vicki had brought.

As they were preparing the meal, Vicki was amazed how easy and fun Ted was to be with. He liked to cook, as did she, so it was very relaxed, almost like they had been together for a long time.

Ted was very attentive to Vicki and she was relaxing with the relationship. She wondered if she could love someone with such a dominant personality. After consuming the scrumptious meal and finishing most of a bottle of chilled chardonnay, Ted took Vicki into his arms and kissed her for the first time.

Vicki felt like she would faint and knew Ted could do anything he wanted with her. He just took her home.

For the first time in several months, and with a smile on her face, Vicki fell asleep with Juno lying next to her.

After a couple of weeks of dating, they were spending all their free time together. One night, after a leisurely dinner at his place, Ted asked Vicki to spend the night. Without hesitating, she agreed.

That night Ted was very attentive, and a gentle and caring lover. Vicki's heart was soaring and she was sure she was falling in love with him.

After Ted was sleeping, she lay awake and wondered what was happening to her. She was so happy, then the voice in her head asked, *why?*

From then on, Vicki and Juno began living at Ted's almost full time. When Ted had to work late or on weekends, *the voice would whisper to her, and she would shush it.* She tried to ignore the nagging thoughts that the inner voice left in her mind.

"Is he really working, or is he seeing someone else?" she asked Juno.

Juno would look up at her and turn her head from side to side as if replying 'who knows?'

*3*

## The Beginning

After dating for only two months, Ted decided that he and Vicki should get married. Vicki thought it might be too soon, when Ted convinced her it was the right time.

"Vicki, we are living together, so I think it's time we got married." said Ted one night right before they went to sleep.

"Don't you think it's a little soon; how do you know you love me? I want to be your wife, and I want it to be forever."

"I think the world of you, and it will last as long as it's good."

Where were those three little words every girl wanted to hear, Vicki asked herself?

She would have to move out of her cottage and wouldn't have the wonderful evenings with just her and Juno. She wanted to be Ted's wife, so, one more time, she put her doubts and *that pesky voice* aside.

They didn't want a large wedding, so one Friday Vicki told Judge Gresham that she and Ted would be in his office at four o'clock that afternoon to be married.

"Bob, Ted and I want you to marry us this afternoon at four o'clock." announced Vicki. "We already have our license and we see no reason to wait."

"Vicki, are you absolutely sure? I told you what I think of Ted. He's a great attorney. I don't think he will be a good husband."

"You don't know him like I do," replied Vicki. "He told me all about his past and says he has changed and is ready to settle down."

"Okay, I'll do it." agreed the Judge, reluctantly.

At four p.m. Vicki and Ted presented themselves to Judge Gresham. Vicki looked stunning in a pale pink top, matching pants and shoes. She carried a bouquet of dark pink roses. Outwardly she appeared relaxed and excited, however, on the inside she was extremely nervous, a feeling she attributed to the wedding jitters.

As usual Ted was in one of his shoe box Brooks Brothers suits. He looked like a fisherman who had just hooked a prize rainbow trout. Would he keep this one?

Barb arrived, feeling upbeat and happy, dressed in a dark pink dress ready to act as Vicki's maid of honor.

Ted's partner, Ben, arrived a few minutes late offering apologies.

The ceremony was short, with only the bride, groom and the two attendants. The Judge wondered where Ted's parents were and why no one else was there. Putting his thoughts aside, he performed the ceremony.

After the ceremony, Ted and Vicki went to their favorite bar for a celebratory drink. As they were toasting each other, a dark haired, exotic looking woman came up to Ted, bent down, and kissed him on the lips.

"Oh, hi Janet, what a surprise. Janet, this is Vicki, Vicki, this is Janet." Ted stammered and immediately rose from his chair to walk Janet back to her table.

Vicki watched Ted talking rapidly and telling Janet that Vicki was his new wife...and *the voice came back and said, Who is she and what is he telling her? Perhaps, you are just a means to an end?*

Vicki teared up and thought to herself, shut up.

Ted returned and kissed Vicki and she thought, *he does love me.*

"So, who is Janet? Do I need to be worried?" asked Vicki trying to smile through the tears.

"She is just a friend from high school and, no, you don't have a thing to worry about."

Told you so, thought Vicki to herself, and later she found out that Ted and Janet had reconnected and broke up about four months earlier. Vicki dismissed it, thinking everyone had relationships in their past.

Ted and Vicki flew to Aspen aboard the firm's private jet and spent their honeymoon in Ted's condo. He hadn't told Vicki about owning a condo in Aspen. Everything had happened so fast, she reasoned that he hadn't thought about it.

They spent two weeks in Aspen sightseeing, eating, enjoying concerts and acting like newlyweds. Vicki was floating on air. Ted began teaching Vicki how to fly fish. She was anxious to learn, since, other than work, fly fishing was Ted's passion.

Ted was on the bank and Vicki was in the middle of the Roaring Fork River trying to keep her footing and cast her fly rod. She slipped on a rock, stepped in a hole and fell head first into the water.

"Don't break the fly rod!" Ted yelled from the bank.

Vicki regained her footing, waded back to the bank and glared at Ted. "You were more worried about this stupid fly rod than you were about me being hurt!" she screamed and stormed off to the car, her waders full of water.

Ted caught up with her and, laughing, said, "Sorry honey, I knew you would be okay, a little wet, but okay."

"It's not funny." Vicki said as she poured water from her waders, got in the car and waited for him.

After they returned from their honeymoon, life seemed to settle down. However, on the first day back to work, Judge Gresham called her into chambers.

"Vicki, we have a problem." he said, looking concerned. "The defense attorneys have filed a motion to disqualify me from hearing the asbestos cases since you are now married to a plaintiffs' attorney."

"Do you want me to quit my job?" Vicki asked sadly.

"No, we need to set some guidelines and see if all the attorneys will agree to them. First, you must agree to never discuss with Ted what you hear in chambers. Second, I don't think you should be in the courtroom during proceedings involving these cases. And, third, you will have no contact with any expert or juror during trials. Do you understand?"

"Yes, however, one of my duties is to be present in the courtroom to assist in setting matters on the docket. Who will do that?" Vicki asked, suddenly feeling guilty for marrying Ted. *The little monster whispered that Ted won't want to be married to you because you won't have access to courtroom information.*

SHUT UP, Vicki screamed silently to herself.

The Judge scheduled a conference with all attorneys involved in the asbestos cases and included Vicki. After some objections and concessions, it was agreed that Vicki would not be present in the courtroom, and she would not divulge any information to counsel. The Judge asked Vicki to agree to these terms, under oath on the record, which she did.

After the conference, Vicki was happy to keep her job, and embarrassed that she was the reason for the problem.

Ted's brother, Charlie, had also married that summer, so their parents had a joint reception at their home to celebrate the nuptials.

Vicki had not met her in-laws until that evening. As she and Ted drove up the long, winding, private lane and Vicki saw the mansion for the first time, she could not believe her eyes. It was one of the largest houses she had ever seen. A large, white tent had been erected on the front lawn where the party would take place.

Vicki thought, what have I got myself into? These people are way above me.

"Good lord, Ted, I had no idea your parents lived in a house like this." she said, her eyes widening with each new view of the property and the house.

"Yes," he said laughing, "I call it the Dracula Mansion."

Ted introduced her to his parents, Henry and Shirley Winter. They hugged her and welcomed her to the family, joking that they would have loved to have been at the wedding. They seemed to understand why they weren't invited, knowing that Ted's impulsive behavior hadn't left time for any planning.

Sensing Vicki's discomfort, Ted's dad took her on a private tour of all three floors of the mansion, which included ten bedrooms, thirteen bathrooms, three full kitchens, several formal living areas and an elevator to the third-floor library. Henry Winter made Vicki feel totally at ease and they became instant friends.

It was a wonderful evening and Vicki quickly felt at home and part of the Winter family.

Fueled by Judge Gresham's question and her own insecurities, Ted's actions before and during their honeymoon, made her wonder. Had Ted married her because he loved her, or, was it for what she could do for him because she worked for the judge hearing all the asbestos cases? She put the question out of her mind, although it would resurface again.

She had always watched her money and this new life was totally foreign to her. When she wasn't working, she and the other partners' wives spent leisurely afternoons lunching and shopping. She told Barb about the excursions and how she couldn't believe how much money the wives spent. This was a totally new lifestyle for Barb, too.

"You wouldn't believe how much money the wives spend on clothes and they are always remodeling their houses. They could do so much good helping the families of the clients."

"Hey, don't complain. You are living the life any of us would want." Barb replied.

Her times with Barb became fewer and fewer. If Ted knew they were planning an outing, he would have something else he wanted Vicki to do, or a place he wanted them to go. He also started complaining about the amount of time she was working. Reluctantly, Vicki decided it was time to quit her job at the court.

Quitting work was a difficult decision, because Vicki had always enjoyed working. However, Ted wanted her to become a partner's wife and devote her life to the marriage and lifestyle he wanted.

After a few months, she became restless and started looking for volunteer opportunities.

Ted said he didn't want Vicki spending her time working or volunteering because he wanted her to be able to travel with him for work and pleasure. So, once again Vicki gave in, although she felt like she was not contributing to society. She tried to keep busy by reading, cooking and shopping. After every shopping trip with the wives, she felt guilty because she bought things she didn't really want and definitely didn't need.

The first business trip Vicki took with Ted was to The Boulders, a resort in Carefree, Arizona for a meeting of asbestos attorneys from all over the country. Vicki met many of the wives and one in particular, Ashley, became a close friend. They spent the days together while their husbands were in meetings.

# 4

# The Wives

Ashley Turner was married to Jason Turner, the first asbestos attorney to reach a multi-million-dollar settlement. Jason and Ashley lived in Westport, Connecticut, where many actors, politicians and old-monied families lived.

Despite the wealth, Ashley was a very caring and down to-earth person. She was petite and had a short pixie haircut, a bubbly personality and sparkling blue eyes. Ashley loved dogs but Jason wouldn't allow any animal in the house. At times, she actually seemed embarrassed about their wealth.

Instantly, Vicki felt at ease with Ashley.

Jason, on the other hand, was narcissistic and very self-centered and selfish. He said unkind things to Ashley.

"Dear, why are you wearing that dress, you know it makes you look wide across the beam." he admonished her.

"Jason, this is one of my favorite dresses. You liked it last time I wore it." Ashley said as she went to change.

Jason and Ashley had three children, all girls, who attended the very best private schools, however, Jason complained that all Ashley had given him were girls.

"Why didn't we have any boys; is there something wrong with you?"

"Of course not; you know the male determines the sex of the child. I had nothing to do with that."

Even though Ashley knew her marriage wasn't perfect, she was determined to stay married because of her children. She was always nervous around Jason, waiting for the next shoe to drop.

She confided in Vicki that she was always dieting, getting facials and exercising because Jason expected a perfect wife, perfect children and a model home.

Sherry Martin was married to Robert Martin and they lived in La Jolla, California. Sherry was a true Southern California girl with long blond hair that had been straightened. She was always tan from spending time on the golf course, tennis court and at the pool. She and Robert had two sons, both of whom were planning to go to law school. Sherry came from a very wealthy family, so the asbestos money didn't mean much to her.

"I know Robert makes a lot of money. His money doesn't affect me one way or the other. My trust fund gives me more money each month than I can ever spend."

Robert and Sherry appeared to have a good, stable marriage, but you never knew what happened behind closed doors.

Francine, Frankie to her friends, was married to Thomas Morgan. They lived in San Francisco on Russian Hill. They had a second home in Vail, Colorado where they spent time in the winter skiing and relaxing in the summer. Frankie's skin was burnished bronze due to her African heritage. She was tall and elegant with a short Afro. When she walked into a room, all eyes turned to look at her.

Thomas reminded everyone of a gladiator, with his athletic build.

Frankie and Thomas did not have children. It was apparent to all that their marriage was in trouble. They stayed as far away from each other as possible when they were in a crowd and when possible, they lived in separate houses.

Frankie had a very successful clothing business and she sold her clothing to high-end boutiques. She started the business before she met Thomas.

"When we were first married, I supported us, so now I am investing my money and living off of Thomas' income." she confided to the group.

Stephanie Goldstein and her husband, Joseph, were older. Stephanie was short and slim with white hair she wore in a short bob. Joseph was "of counsel" to several of the asbestos firms, having earned his stripes on other types of products liability cases.

Stephanie was energetic for her age and Vicki immediately felt that Stephanie was the mother she had always wanted. Stephanie felt that Vicki was one of her daughters.

Stephanie and Joseph lived on Star Island, Florida and had a condo on Maui, Hawaii for their getaway. They had three sons, one daughter and seven grandchildren. Family was obviously their main focus.

The topic of a girls' getaway came up over lunch. They all agreed it was a great idea and would be fun. Vicki was thrilled to be included in the group.

"Hey, we all get along so well, why don't we do a girls' week sometime? Our husbands work such long hours, we need an escape where we can just relax and do girl things." Ashley suggested.

"What a great idea." Frankie said. "What fun," chimed in Sherry.

"Do you want an old broad to tag along?" asked Stephanie. "I am so happy you include me in your group."

"Yes, Stephanie, I can't imagine you not being here. Hey, why don't we call ourselves the asbestos wives?" Vicki exclaimed, excited and happy.

On the plane home, Vicki told Ted about the possible girls' getaway and he immediately thought it was a good idea.

"Great idea, where are you going, when and for how long?" he asked, enthusiastically.

"Nothing is final yet, we'll talk more on the phone soon and start making plans. You almost act excited to get rid of me for a while?"

"Not at all dear. It's just that I will be spending much more time getting ready for trials. In fact, we are going to hire an associate just for the asbestos cases and a couple of paralegals to help out."

This was the first Vicki heard about Ted hiring more staff and felt shut out of his life. *Hello red flag. Vicki immediately shut it out...*

In spite of feeling a little sad that Ted would hire more staff, the trip had been a great experience for Vicki. She met the other asbestos wives, and they began planning their getaway. When he wasn't in meetings, she and Ted had had a good time, eating, making love and attempting to play golf. He was trying to teach Vicki how to play golf. His impatience came through if she didn't do what he thought she should do. Vicki vowed she would take lessons.

After one particularly fulfilling session of sex, Vicki approached the subject of children. In spite of her earlier proclamation, she had been thinking about having a child with Ted. After all, they were in their thirties, had plenty of money and a beautiful home in which to raise children. It would be so much fun to have a child, and a funny, loving husky, to grow up together.

"It's too early to talk about this. I'm not sure I want children and I want you available when I need you." Ted said, a little too firmly.

Once again, Vicki felt she had brought up a taboo subject and didn't mention children again. She wanted to be the mother she never had realizing that this would have to wait.

# 5

## Sea Island

Soon after the meeting at The Boulders, the asbestos attorney group had another meeting. This time the meeting was at The Cloisters, Sea Island, Georgia. Vicki went with Ted and on arrival looked for Ashley.

The setting was beautiful. Ted and Vicki had a large suite, complete with butler service. Vicki wanted to have a cocktail party for the group.

"Ted, what do you think about inviting everyone to our suite for cocktails before dinner tomorrow night, it would probably cost a lot?"

"Sounds like a great idea, don't worry about the cost, we can afford it."

The next day Vicki and Ashley arranged for the food and liquor through the catering department, then went to the beach to find Sherry, Frankie and Stephanie. Immediately, the talk turned to the girls' week. The more they talked the more accepted Vicki felt. As soon as she was with Ted the old insecurities popped up again.

The night of the party every lawyer and his wife or

significant other arrived dressed to the nines. Vicki had chosen a long white skirt and top, turquoise belt and jewelry. The food was wonderful and the service was definitely worthy of the five-star rating of the resort.

Somehow, dinner was forgotten, the party lasting into the morning hours.

The next day, Vicki received many compliments and thanks for a great party. She was floating on cloud nine. Even Ted complimented her.

Hugging her, he said, "Honey, the party last night was wonderful. You are a great hostess, in addition to being beautiful. I am so proud of you."

"Thank you, sweetie," she replied, her spirits soaring and her eyes shining.

That night, Jason, Ashley, Ted and Vicki went to dinner at a very high-end restaurant at the resort. Vicki started noticing traits in Ted that she found repulsive in Jason, and the more wine Ted drank, the more abusive he became. Vicki tried to ignore the comments and figured she would adjust to Ted's quirks over time. After all, she had never been exposed to the lifestyle she found herself living, and assumed Ted was reacting to the pressures of the job.

After they returned to their suite, Vicki went right to bed and turned her back to Ted.

"Hey, want's wrong with you?"

"You really hurt me when you told Jason and Ashley that you had rescued me, a poor little lost girl. I don't feel I needed rescuing."

"Sorry, guess I had too much wine." Ted said turning over and pretending to be asleep.

As the wives were sitting around the pool or on the

beach, Vicki had a feeling that under all the smiles and expensive clothes there were some unhappy and abused wives. The husbands were lord and master of their universe, and the wives were there to raise the children, keep a perfect home, entertain well and look pretty.

On the last day at Sea Island, the five wives had lunch and began planning their retreat. They decided Key West would be a fun place to go in the winter. They could get sun, play golf, tennis, shop and just spend time away from home. Ashley volunteered to find available resorts.

"I'll look for a nice resort that will cater to our needs. Also, I think we should do it the first part of November, before the holidays." she said.

"I think we should all mark our calendars for the last week in October and the first week in November." remarked Sherry.

The other wives agreed, and with that, the retreat plans were put into action.

After lunch, the wives went to the pool and continued discussing the first outing of the asbestos wives. Ashley told the group that she and Jason were building a house on the beach in Malibu. She said future getaways could be at that house; Frankie volunteered their house in Vail; Stephanie said they definitely had to spend time at their house on Maui. After more discussion, they decided that for their first trip they would go to Key West where they could all be guests.

After Ted and Vicki returned home, Vicki and Ashley talked on the phone at least once a week about the trip and shared confidences.

"Sometimes Jason can be so mean," Ashley complained. "Nothing I do is right and now he is talking about politics.

For sure, I don't want a life in politics."

"I know what you are talking about. Sometimes I don't know who Ted is. He can change moods at the snap of a finger and it scares me." Vicki confided.

During a conference call with all the wives, the dates for their retreat were agreed on. Ashley made the reservations at a very posh resort/spa. After they all agreed to meet at the Miami airport at four p.m. on November first, Vicki made her plane reservations. For the first time in her life she would fly first class. Sherry arranged for a limo to pick them up at the Miami airport, take them to their hotel, and to Key West the next morning.

Vicki thought Ted seemed a little too happy about the trip, so she didn't dwell on it. She was looking forward to seven days with the other wives, knowing she would miss Ted. Would he miss her?

"Honey, thank you for letting me go on this trip. It will be fun. I will really miss you. You will take care of Juno, won't you?"

"You will have a great time. Of course, I will take care of Juno. She is my second favorite girl."

Ted walked out of the room just as Vicki asked, "Will you miss me?"

*Damn, there was that figure behind the little voice with the red flag.*

She fought back tears and started thinking about clothes for the trip.

Although Ted drove Vicki to the airport and said all the right words, Vicki felt he acted like he had a much more important matter to attend to.

"Can I just drop you at curbside check in?" he asked.

"Sure, except I was hoping you could come in for a glass of wine before I leave." she said, feeling a surge of panic.

"No can do,"

After Ted dropped her, she suddenly realized she felt a sense of relief to be away from him. Then she felt guilty because she was relieved to be away from him after only three months of marriage. *Go Away little voice!*

Waiting for her flight in the first-class lounge, she tried to call Ted. His cell went to voice mail. She called his office and his secretary answered.

"Hi Sandy, is Ted in?"

"Hi Vicki, no he's marked out for the afternoon. Do you want me to have him call you if he calls in?"

"No, I just wanted to say goodbye again, thanks.

Vicki had ordered a lemon drop martini and after the calls, she had another one, trying to relax. By the time she boarded the plane, she had decided she would not call Ted again, hoping he would call her.

# 6

## Key West

Vicki's plane landed at the Miami airport at two-thirty in the afternoon on November first. She retrieved her luggage and went to the first-class lounge to wait until four when the wives had agreed to meet.

She had a glass of chardonnay while waiting and tried to read the novel she had on her Kindle. Her cell phone felt like a huge rock in the pocket of her jacket. She checked voice mail, and there was no message from Ted.

I will not call him. I will not call him, she told herself and then dialed his cell phone anyway. Again, it went to voice mail. She didn't leave a message. Why did I call him she thought, chastising herself?

Finally, four o'clock arrived and the wives met at baggage claim.

"I feel like my little family is together again." grinned Stephanie.

"It is so good to see you all, it's been way too long." said Sherry looking tan and like Southern California.

"Ladies, this is going to be so much fun." Frankie said, looking absolutely stunning as usual.

"This has to become a yearly, or better yet, twice yearly event; away from husbands who work too much, kids and houses." Ashley chimed in.

"I didn't think today would ever come." Vicki said smiling, even though she was hurting from no phone call from Ted.

The wives found their limo, piled in and quickly drank the bottle of chilled champagne waiting for them.

Stephanie had made the reservations for their one night in Miami. She had reserved the Venus Suite at the very posh Versace Mansion. "As the unofficial mother of this group, tonight's room and dinner are my treat." she told them.

"No," the other four said at the same time.

"No arguing, I insist," said Stephanie.

They had a suite with two bedrooms and a sofa bed in the living area. They changed into beach clothes and left the hotel for the first night of their adventure.

They walked on the beach, and then decided to have drinks and eat dinner at II Sole in the Mansion. They enjoyed a scrumptious dinner of fresh fish, salad, fruit and key lime pie for dessert. Of course, chardonnay was also consumed.

"I am so full; I don't think I'll eat the rest of the week." Vicki said, licking her lips.

"Okay, we'll just drink, so it will be a liquid diet." laughed Ashley.

They went to their suite and ordered more wine from room service. They sat on the balcony overlooking Ocean Drive, and admired the view. Each, in her own mind, was thinking about home and what was happening in their lives. They realized how lucky they were to have this time away.

Except for superficial comments about the upcoming week, there wasn't much conversation that night. Once again, they were shy, bashful, school girls.

"I know we are going to have such a great time." Ashley commented.

"Yes, we are," agreed Sherry.

"I'm just glad to be away from the shop and all the other commitments." Frankie said.

"I hope Ted remembers I'm his wife." lamented Vicki.

"Oh, just wait until tomorrow night. We'll be giggling and gossiping like sorority sisters." smiled Stephanie.

Each wife secretly envied Stephanie and her stable, happy life. She and Joe were definitely partners.

Once Vicki was in bed, she looked at her cell phone. No call from Ted. Telling herself he was just working late, she tried to go to sleep. After tossing and turning for two hours, she turned the cell phone off. She finally drifted off to sleep.

The alarm woke her way too early the next morning. She went to the balcony and joined the other wives who were having breakfast.

Vicki had a cup of coffee and decided to take a second cup back to her room. Once there, she turned her phone on, expecting to see a message from Ted. Nothing.

Damn him. I'll show him, she thought as she turned the phone off again.

At eleven a.m. the limo arrived at the hotel. The wives got in and off they went to Key West.

They checked into their bungalow at the resort, se-lected their bedrooms, changed into their swimming suits and went to the beach, where they found lounge chairs and a very handsome attendant to keep them supplied with towels and lovely tropical drinks with little umbrellas.

"Wow, will you look at that hunk," teased Frankie. "I just lost my wedding ring."

"Oh honey, I think I'm in love." Ashley blushed.

"I think I'll adopt him." Stephanie laughed.

"We don't have anything like that in California." Sherry added.

"Sure, would be fun to make Ted jealous." Vicki said, only half joking.

The attendant was dark and dangerous looking, with jet black hair, dark eyes and muscles that he obviously en-joyed showing off for the ladies.

"Hello gorgeous ladies, what can I do for you?" he asked, emphasizing "do."

Vicki blushed and jokingly said, "Make my husband jeal-ous."

"It would be my pleasure; my name is Ramon." he an-swered as he kissed Vicki's hand.

"Oh, you tease," Vicki said regaining her com-posure.

After the wives had ordered their umbrella cocktails, Ashley said, "Vicki, don't you need lotion on your back? I'm sure Ramon would be glad to do it."

"Yeah, I'm sure he would, but I love my husband." re-plied Vicki.

Vicki felt the wives loosening up and beginning to relax. She felt like they were in paradise. She was sure Ted loved her and would never cheat on her.

*But the figure was waving the red flag, and voice was screaming in her ear. Be realistic. He hasn't returned your call. Too bad Juno can't talk, she knows what is going on.*

To forget about Ted and smiling up at Ramon, Vicki ordered a second cocktail.

Ashley asked Vicki how she and Ted got together. Vicki told them how they had met, the fast courtship, the quick wedding, and all about Ted's family. All four wives said it was so romantic, then Vicki noticed that Stephanie did not act quite as excited as the others.

*Again, the demon raised its ugly head. She was hoping to feel more secure about her marriage after spending time with the other wives, so she told the voice to go away.*

She also told the wives about her childhood and the abuse she and Anna suffered.

"Oh, I'm so sorry Vicki, no child should live in fear of their parent." said Ashley.

Sherry and Frankie agreed with Ashley.

Stephanie actually had tears running down her face as she said, "I wish you had been my daughter. You are beautiful, kind, gentle and talented. You didn't deserve that and neither did your sister."

Vicki smiled back through her own tears, "Thank you all; at least I know I am loved now."

They said their goodbyes to Ramon and told him that they would see him the next day.

"Rest well ladies," he said.

"Well, obviously, he's a shill for the resort." laughed Vicki, and she added, "Be nice to the ladies and the resort will make more money."

That evening, they had a quiet dinner at a seafood restaurant on the resort grounds, then went back to their bungalow to get settled, agreeing to meet on the patio for a nightcap.

They were much more relaxed that night and began to open up about their marriages.

"Jason becomes so distant at times. I attribute it to trial preparation or just too much work, although, lately he's been staying at the office way too long. The good thing is, I don't think he would divorce me because it would cost him too much money." said Ashley.

"Ashley, you don't really think he's running around on you, do you?" asked Vicki.

"Don't know, and don't want to think about it during our wonderful week." said Ashley and then continued, "You know, twelve years ago, when we were first married, we were completely involved in starting our family and planning our future together. Then once Jason started working on the asbestos cases, he became a different person."

"Now, I feel like a military wife whose husband is always away on deployment, except I have plenty of money. Every time I go to Jason's office, his associate, Charlotte, is always there on Jason's side of the desk. Jason says he is mentoring Char, as he calls her. I try not to worry, but I do." confessed Ashley.

Then, Vicki told them about Janet. "You know, after our wedding, Ted and I stopped at our favorite bar for a drink and this broad came up to him and kissed him. He walked off with her, obviously upset and embarrassed. My heart actually sank. But then, he came back to our table, and off we went to Aspen, where we had a wonderful time on our honeymoon. Later, I found out that the woman was a former flame and they had just broken up four months before."

"I don't think you have anything to worry about, you are beautiful and talented. Why would Ted want to stray?" asked Stephanie.

It was Sherry's turn. "I grew up with a father who worked all the time and didn't have much time for family. I swore I would never marry a man who was like that and look at me. My mother and I were extremely close and she got me involved in La Jolla society. After she died, I continued to be involved, except there was something lacking. As you know, La Jolla is very upscale so most society events benefit that sector of society, not the people who really need help. I don't spend any time at Bob's office. I want our family to spend more time together, especially once our boys are married and have children."

Vicki immediately felt that Sherry and Bob had a loveless marriage, and she wondered to herself, if this is what happens to the wives of asbestos attorneys.

Frankie said, "I admit I'm not happy in my marriage, however, my business keeps me so busy I have very little time for Tom. Since we have two homes, we can easily avoid each other except on the few occasions we have to be together. I know Tom has had affairs, and so have I."

Vicki could tell Frankie was putting up a strong front, while she was hurting inside. Money can't buy love and respect.

Then, Stephanie told her story. "Joe and I have had our problems, believe me. Shortly after our first baby was born, Joe had an affair. He was becoming quite successful so I told him I would take all his money and his child and leave. It took a long time to get over the hurt of him being unfaithful, but now he is totally devoted to our family. We both put family first and it is working. I wish you all had such confidence in your marriages.

I'm here for you anytime. Joe and I will be celebrating forty-years of marriage next year. I want you and your husbands there. Your hubbies can see what stability is like."

Vicki noticed that Stephanie smiled every time she mentioned Joe.

Oh, how I wish I had that, thought Vicki.

After the wives retired for the evening, Vicki kept replaying their conversations and wondered, except for Stephanie, if any of them were truly happy?

A thought stirred in the back of Vicki's mind...what if the wives could do something for their husbands' asbestos clients?

Where did that come from? she thought. Hmm, I'll think about it more later.

Vicki kept the phone by her bed and when Ted hadn't called by one a.m., she decided to call him, since it was only eleven p.m. in Stone Mountain. Once again, his phone went to voice mail. *The little voice started shouting in her head and she slept very little.*

I can't tell the others about this, it makes me cry and I don't want to ruin our trip, she thought.

The next morning, they ordered breakfast in the bungalow, each secretly hoping Ramon would deliver it. Breakfast arrived without Ramon. They agreed to have a quiet, relaxing day with some shopping later on. There was an uneasiness among them, and except for Stephanie, each was afraid they had revealed too much the night before. As the morning wore on, they all relaxed and concentrated on having a good time.

Vicki went to her room to dress for the day and her phone showed a message. Her heart soared.

"Hi Vicki, it's Ted -who else- sorry I haven't called. It has been wild this week. Tomorrow, I have to go to Johns Mansville headquarters in Colorado and look at documents. I'm taking my new associate, Julie, so she can start learning the ropes. I'll try to call you tonight. Talk to you later."

*"JULIE!" the little voice said. Go away. I don't want to think about it.*

Where were those three words, or, I miss you?

The wives had lunch at a very upscale restaurant that specialized in stone crab. The food and wine were wonderful. Then they went shopping. Vicki had never been in such expensive shops or seen such beautiful clothes.

"I have never been in shops like this. No-way can I buy clothes that cost that much."

"Oh honey, we'll teach you the ropes." laughed Frankie. "I know clothes and with your great body, you can wear anything."

The other wives laughed as they rang the bell on the door of a very posh boutique.

"What, you have to ring the bell to get in?"

Vicki asked.

"Yes, and you have to have an appointment." said Sherry. "Luckily, Frankie knows people."

Once inside, Vicki found a cocktail dress she loved. When she looked at the price tag, she let out a gasp, "Three-thousand dollars for a dress! I would never pay that for something I wouldn't wear often."

In unison, the wives said "Oh yes you will, try it on."

Frankie took Vicki and the dress into a dressing room. When Vicki pulled the dress over her head and saw herself in the mirror, she couldn't believe her eyes.

"Wow, olive green is definitely a great color on you." said Frankie. "Let's show the others."

When Vicki walked out of the dressing room, she felt like royalty.

"Wow, ladies, I feel gorgeous and sexy." she said.

"Yes, you are, and you have to buy that dress." the wives said.

"How can I possibly spend this much money? Ted will have a fit."

Then she remembered Ted's call and who the hell is Julie? She felt that she deserved something for the hurt she was feeling.

"OK, I'm going to buy it." she smiled. "Now I need shoes, onward and upward."

After all the wives had made special purchases, they went back to the resort and decided dinner would be at the very fancy restaurant at the resort, so they could wear their new clothes.

When the wives walked into the restaurant, all eyes turned their way and conversation seemed to stop. Vicki had never felt more beautiful.

"Good evening ladies," the host said. "I'm going to put you at the best table in the house so everyone can see you. You are definitely going to help sales tonight."

After they were seated, Frankie said, "Good lord, can you believe the staff here. I think they are all gorgeous and really suck up."

After a dinner of fresh seafood, salad, wine and more wine, the wives went back to their bungalow. Vicki went to her room to change into pajamas and had a message from Ted.

"Hi Honey, I'm in Denver. I will call from the hotel. Hope you are having a great time, love you."

Well, the two words were almost as fulfilling as the three words.

Vicki joined the other wives on the patio and they re-hashed the day. It had been a great day for Vicki and she told them so. She kept her phone with her waiting for Ted's call from the hotel.

The wives decided the next morning, they would make a tee time for the following day and arrange to rent golf clubs. Tomorrow would be a beach and pool day.

Vicki went to her room, left her phone on and actually slept well. The next morning, she chastised herself because she was so dependent on Ted's call to make her day good or not so good.

The wives went to the beach, each wearing a new swim-suit they bought the day before.

Vicki's suit was a bright orange two-piece that showed off her stunning, tan figure. She wore big gold earrings, bracelets and her four-carat engagement ring. She did look great and she knew it. If only Ted could see me now, she thought.

Ramon was immediately at her side, offering to put lotion on her back. She politely refused and the other wives all laughed.

"Hey, if you don't want him, I'll take him." Frankie said.

"You can have him; I am faithful to Ted." Vicki replied, thinking of Julie again.

They all relaxed with their umbrella drinks and books. It was a quiet afternoon and Vicki felt so happy with her friends. About three-thirty they decided to go back to the bungalow, shower and have dinner from room service.

"This is so much fun," said Ashley. "I do hope we do it again soon."

"For sure," said Vicki and laughing said, "I'm all for a getaway every other month."

The others agreed they needed a getaway twice a year. Dinner was ordered, along with two bottles of chardonnay.

"All five wives drink the same wine," observed Vicki.

"Just shows that this group was meant to be." said Sherry.

"Hey, how about a getaway in Napa?" asked Frankie. "The wine train is supposed to be so much fun."

"Well, my son happens to own a vineyard in Napa with a gorgeous house. I'm sure we could stay there." said Stephanie.

"All right, it's a date," said Ashley. "We'll coordinate dates and details later."

"I'll check with John for next spring." said Stephanie.

Vicki said, "I am so lucky to be part of this group. I'll check with Ted."

"Don't check, just tell him," said Frankie.

Sure, Vicki thought, you don't like your husband, I love mine.

After a day of sun and wine, they retired to their rooms

early that night. No call from Ted. Vicki turned her phone off and went to sleep.

The next morning, the five of them had a tee time for nine thirty, so they had the hotel shuttle take them to the golf course.

"You guys, I have just started playing so please be patient." said Vicki.

"Don't worry, we're playing for fun." said Sherry.

They played as a threesome and a twosome. Vicki shared a cart with Ashley. All five women wore stylish golf outfits.

Vicki wore a violet skort, a white, sleeveless golf shirt, a violet visor, and white golf shoes. She felt like a million dollars.

She played well and enjoyed playing with the ladies much more than playing with Ted. Following a twinge of guilt, she relaxed.

After a day on the course, they were tired and didn't want to dress up for dinner so they ate at the golf club. They called the resort for a ride back and were surprised when the driver was Ramon. He opened the back door of the SUV for the ladies, and Vicki was the last one in. As she entered, Ramon whispered, "I would love to see you alone. Will you meet me tonight in the main bar? Let me know when we get back to the resort."

Vicki was blushing when she took her seat in the SUV. The others looked at her with that knowing look, yet no one said anything.

When they got back to their resort Vicki took him aside and told Ramon, "I am a newlywed and I love my husband. Thank you for the invitation, I'll have to say no."

She felt so much better after setting the record straight with Ramon. He was still attentive as he shifted his attention to Frankie as his favorite.

Once again, they all changed into pajamas and ordered wine.

"Hey ladies, do you realize we didn't talk about our husbands at all today. Let's not ruin a good thing. What do we want to do with our lives after children?" asked Ashley.

"I don't think I will have kids," said Vicki. "There is something I've been thinking about. Our husbands' clients are really struggling dealing with the illness, lawsuit, family and day-to-day living. We all have so much free time. Why don't we do something for these victims?" asked Vicki.

"Might, it be a good idea," said Frankie. "The stores are running themselves because of my great staff. I'm sure I could help."

"You know," said Stephanie "I've been thinking about doing good for years, then, something always comes up. Maybe if we put our heads together, we can think of something."

"I'm in," said Sherry. "I'm too tired to think about it tonight. Let's talk about it later. Tomorrow is our last day here; I think we should do a last beach day."

"Okay," they all agreed and went to bed.

Vicki got into bed, didn't look at her phone and immediately went to sleep.

The next day, they went to the beach. Ramon was nowhere to be seen.

"Maybe it's his day off." said Sherry.

Vicki was actually relieved. She didn't want to see him

and she didn't want to see Frankie do anything stupid.

They went to the main restaurant at the resort for dinner, then to the bungalow and each went to their room to pack and go to bed.

There was a message on Vicki's phone. "Hi Kiddo, I'm home from Denver. Very productive trip. Let me know what time you want me to pick you up tomorrow." said Ted.

Vicki called him back and he answered the phone. "Hi Sweetie. I have sure missed you, and oh yes, Juno too." Vicki laughed, relieved he answered his phone.

"What time do you get in?" he asked.

"My flight lands at five-forty-five tomorrow evening. Let's go to dinner after you pick me up."

"OK, see you then."

"I love you," Vicki said.

"Me too," he replied.

Well, that wasn't very satisfying, Vickie thought.

The next morning, the wives had a leisurely breakfast in the bungalow. Once again, no Ramon. When they checked out, the SUV was waiting. "Good morning ladies, my name is Daniel and I will be taking you to the airport."

They got in the SUV and were quiet on the way to Miami. When they got to the airport, they said their goodbyes.

"This was so great," said Sherry. "Let me know what I can do to help with Napa."

"Just remember ladies, I am always here for you." said Stephanie, giving Vicki an extra hug.

"We are so lucky," said Vicki. "I'm going to miss you all so much."

"Don't forget me when you plan Napa." Frankie said.

"No way," laughed Ashley. "We are officially "the asbestos wives" as Vicki named us."

Vicki boarded her plane and once again felt a foreboding that she didn't want to think about. She kept reliving the past week as she tried to sleep.

Ted was waiting for her with roses and Vicki's spirits lifted, thinking to herself, he does love me after all of my worrying.

After they kissed, they retrieved her luggage, got into the Range Rover and went to their favorite steak house for dinner.

That night, Ted took Vicki in his arms. They made love and went to sleep holding each other.

Juno slept in her bed by Vicki's side of the bed. I sure hope no one else has slept in our bed, thought Vicki suddenly. Now, where did that come from?

## 7

## *Life Back to Normal*

When Vicki woke up the next morning, she realized it was her first holiday season with Ted. She needed to start planning immediately. First, however, she would take a walk around the island with Juno.

The sun was shining and the weather was warm for November. She hadn't thought about Ted since she got up that morning. She felt a twinge of guilt and yet a sense of freedom.

"Wonder what time he left the house?" she asked Juno, and added," If only you could talk."

When Vicki returned from her walk, she checked her cell phone. What she saw made her smile. There was a text message from Ashley.

"What a great week, miss you all already."

Another text from Frankie, "Wish it were last week."

And one from Sherry, "What fun, very special time with very special ladies."

"Miss my girls," from Stephanie.

Vicki texted back to all four with, "I am ready to do another week, right now."

Then, Vicki called Ted's mom to see what they do for the holidays.

"Hi Vicki, Honey, how was your week away?" asked Shirley.

"It was great. We're going to get away more often. I think the guys like it too. What I really called about are the holidays. Do you have family traditions?"

"Oh, well, no. We really don't plan anything special. It seems Ted is always busy or away. Maybe now would be a good time to start some. What do you have in mind?"

"I don't know. For sure, I would like to do something on the island. Why don't you think about it and we'll talk in a couple of days and decide?"

"Sounds wonderful, talk to you later this week."

After the call with Shirley, Vicki decided she needed to see what groceries were in the cabin and probably go to the store. When she opened the refrigerator, she saw an open bottle of red wine.

When did Ted start drinking red wine? *Maybe he didn't drink it, or maybe he shared it, the voice said.*

Vicki's mood immediately changed and she sat down and cried.

What is wrong with me? Why can't I totally trust Ted? Has he found someone new? she asked herself.

The more she thought about it, the worse she felt. To make herself feel better she dialed Ted's number.

"Hi Vicki, how was your trip?" asked Sandy.

"It was great Sandy, is Ted there?"

"No, he and Julie had a deposition this morning. They should be back in the office any time. May I have him call?"

"No thanks, I'll try his cell."

Vicki sat in silence staring out the window at the lake.

Finally, Juno came up and nudged her hand.

"Hello sweet girl," Vicki said scratching Juno behind the ears. "What should I do?"

At that minute, the phone rang. It was Barb and not Ted. "Hi traveler, how was the trip?" she asked.

"Hi Barb," Vicki said, trying to hide the tears. "It was wonderful. I really enjoy the wives, although you are still my go-to person."

"You don't sound good, what's going on?" asked Barb.

"Nothing, just feeling a little insecure after seeing an opened bottle of wine in the refrigerator. Ted doesn't drink red wine."

"Don't worry about anything, he loves you," said Barb with a little hesitance in her voice. "Why don't we do lunch tomorrow?"

"Okay, I really need a friend now, see you tomorrow."

Vicki decided to make Ted a special dinner. She called the marina and asked Harvey to bring the boat over so she could go to the store. Living on the island could be inconvenient but the peace and quiet made it worth it.

While she waited for Harvey and the boat, she changed into warm clothes and made her grocery list.

Harvey arrived and she got in the boat and off they went. It hadn't been cold enough for the lake to freeze. Luckily, she had her BMW Z4 in a garage at the marina, so she had wheels once they got to the mainland.

At the store, she bought salad, filets, asparagus, baking potatoes, and cheesecake for dessert. She called Ted and asked him to let her know when he would be home, so she could have her special dinner ready. Harvey took her back to the island.

"We really need to get another boat." said Vicki.

"No problem, Miss Vicki," answered Harvey.

Back home, Vicki showered, styled her hair and dressed in a black top and pants. The top was low cut and showed off her figure and tan.

She went to the kitchen and started preparing the dinner. She made a Caesar salad and put it in the refrigerator to keep it cold. She set the dining table near the tall glass sliding doors so they could look out on the lake.

It was five-thirty, and she still hadn't heard from Ted, so she called his cell.

"Hi Sweetie, it's five-thirty and I almost have dinner ready. When will you be home?"

At eight-thirty she sat by the fireplace with tears running down her face. What was going on? Who is he with?

Juno jumped up on the sofa and put her head in Vicki's lap. Vicki broke down and sobbed into Juno's thick fur.

Finally, at ten o'clock Vicki went to bed. If she were on the mainland, she would get in her car with Juno and drive away from this life.

About two a.m. she felt Ted's side of the bed move. "Where have you been?" she asked crying.

"Don't start with me Vicki."

She turned over and cried herself to sleep. When she woke up the next morning, Ted was gone.

What am I going to do? she asked herself.

At eleven o'clock she threw on jeans and a top, ran a brush through her hair and called Harvey.

"This is ridiculous," she told Harvey. "Would you find a boat for me? It doesn't have to be fancy like this one, just one I can use to come and go as I please."

"Miss Vicki, I just happen to have a nice little boat that would be perfect for you. Do you want me to ask the owner how much he wants for it?" Harvey asked.

"No, just buy it by the time I get back from lunch. Tell the owner I can transfer money into his account today." Then she drove to the restaurant to meet Barb.

"What in the hell happened to you?" Barb asked.

"Oh, Barb," replied Vicki crying. "Ted was out until two this morning and I cooked a very romantic dinner. He didn't even call."

"Listen sweetie, I shouldn't tell you this but I love you and I think you should know. James and I were eating at the marina Friday night and we saw Ted and some young blond get in his boat and head to the island."

"What am I going to do?" cried Vicki.

"I think you need to see a psychologist or psychiatrist and second, the best divorce attorney you can find. Not that you're going to get a divorce but you need to explore your options."

"I don't know Barb," Vicki said. "I must be doing something wrong. I just can't seem to please him anymore."

"It's not you," said Barb. "He's always been an ass bandit and can't seem to change."

The waiter came to take their order and Vicki immediately ordered a vodka on the rocks. While they were eating, Vicki's phone rang. It was Ted. "Hi Hon, sorry about last night. It was the day from hell. We are having an emergency meeting of the asbestos attorneys tomorrow through Saturday. Are you up for a trip to San Francisco?"

"Of course, Sweetheart," beamed Vicki.

"Oh Barb, we are going to San Francisco tomorrow." clamored Vicki. "Guess I was just being my insecure self."

"Good," said Barb, not looking at Vicki.

After lunch Vicki went back to the marina where Harvey showed her the boat.

"I love it," said Vicki. "How much is it?"

"I got him down to six-hundred dollars," said Harvey. "I paid him so you wouldn't have to go through the hassle."

"Thank you so much Harvey. Do you want cash or can I write you a check?"

"Don't worry about it Miss Vicki, I'll put it on your monthly bill."

"Great. Is the boat ready?"

"Sure is."

Vicki boarded the boat, started the engine and went home. She had a sense of freedom she seldom felt. Her husband loved her after all and she had her own boat.

When she got home, she showered, called the Martins to see if they wanted Juno for a few days. This time she took extra time with packing. She was going to keep her husband happy. She thought about calling the wives, but they would be in San Francisco.

When Ted got home, they gathered their luggage and Juno. As they boarded the Chris Craft Ted asked, "Who's boat?"

"Mine," beamed Vicki. "Harvey knew the guy who wanted to sell it, so I got it for six-hundred dollars. Now,

I won't have to call Harvey to come and get me all the time."

"I wish you had asked me first. I know Harvey doesn't mind getting you back to the mainland." Ted said, sounding irritated.

"Sorry, I acted on impulse," apologized Vicki.

"We'll talk about it later," said Ted, ending the conversation.

They dropped Juno at the Martin's and she immediately ran to the cottage. The Martins had not rented the cottage again. Vicki paid them each month so she and Ted could use it if the weather was so bad, they couldn't get back to the island. So far, it hadn't been used but Vicki felt good knowing it was there when needed.

Once they boarded the firm's plane and were in the air, Ted started working and Vicki tried to read but felt the icy elephant in the plane.

"Ted, I'm sorry. I had no idea the boat would upset you." said Vicki. "I just thought it would be easier for me to get to the mainland."

"I don't want to talk about it. You did what you did, so be it." Ted glared at her. "I need to know where you are all the time in case, I need you to do something for me."

The rest of the trip was spent in stony silence. So much for a romantic trip thought Vicki.

When the plane landed and they were on their way to the hotel, Vicki touched Ted's hand and he pulled away.

Oh, what have I done? thought Vicki. Why can't I be the wife he wants me to be. I wouldn't blame him if he found someone else. Someone prettier and smarter.

They checked into their room and Ted said some of the

guys were already there so he was going down to the bar.

"I'll go with and maybe Ashley or some of the other wives will be there." said Vicki.

When they got to the bar Vicki saw Jason, however, Ashley wasn't there.

"Jason, so good to see you, where is Ashley?" asked Vicki.

"She's not here. I would like for you to meet Charlotte." answered Jason.

The first thing Vicki noticed was Charlotte's hand on Jason's arm. Look at that diamond; she must be engaged to some really rich guy, thought Vicki.

Vicki glanced over Jason's shoulder and saw Stephanie. She excused herself and went to talk to her.

"Vicki, I have something to tell you. Even though it has not been a month since our getaway, Jason has left Ashley and is engaged to Charlotte." said Stephanie, putting her arm around Vicki.

"That asshole!" said Vicki a little too loud. People turned and stared.

"What happened?" she asked Stephanie, visibly shaking.

"It seems Jason has been with Charlotte for quite some time. Ashley tried to put up a brave front, but the marriage fell apart after our trip to Florida. The good thing, she will get millions in the divorce settlement."

"Oh, Stephanie, what can we do for her?" asked Vicki.

"We'll call her tomorrow to cheer her up and maybe plan another get together right after the holidays."

"Good idea."

"Now, what's happening with you?" asked Stephanie. "You look exhausted and sad."

"Things just aren't great right now." replied Vicki.

Later that night when she and Ted were back in their room, Vicki put on a sexy negligee.

"Did you buy that for anyone special?" he asked.

"For you, and you only," answered Vicki.

"Sorry, I'm so exhausted, I just want to sleep." Ted said.

Dejected, Vicki sat up reading most of the night. She texted Ashley and told her how sorry she was because she and Jason had split.

"Vicki, it's sad but you can't believe the freedom I feel. I have plenty of money and am going to sell this house and move to the house in Malibu when it's finished. Maybe I'll stand taller and let my hair grow so I'll look like Sherry." Ashley said, trying to act happy.

"Ashley, you are talking to me, remember." replied Vicki. "Stephanie suggested we have a girls' get away soon after the first of the year."

"Great, I'm up for that. My parents will come and stay with the girls."

"We're going to call you tomorrow; we'll talk then." texted Vicki.

Suddenly, Vicki thought I haven't called Shirley about the holidays. I have to get a hold of myself and get things back to normal. But, what does Ted want? Vicki thought to herself.

After very little sleep, Vicki called Stephanie's room the next morning and suggested they meet for breakfast later. Then, she called Shirley.

"Shirley, I am so sorry I didn't call before we left. Ted

had an emergency meeting in San Francisco and we'll be here until Saturday. So sorry I didn't call you when I said I would."

"Vicki, Honey, don't worry about it." replied Shirley "We are used to Ted's lifestyle. We are having Thanksgiving dinner with friends and I've been thinking about Christmas. How about a joint party? If the weather is nice, we could do it on the island, and if not, we can do it here."

"Sounds great, I promise I will call you next week so we can make plans."

When Vicki met Stephanie for breakfast, she told her about the texts with Ashley the night before.

"Oh, Stephanie, I am just devastated for Ashley." said Vicki, her eyes filling with tears.

"Ashley will be fine, in fact, I bet she's happier. You're the one I'm worried about. As you are well aware, you are my favorite. Come on, tell me what is going on."

"I don't know, Stephanie. Ted was fine when I first got home and now, he's so distant and staying at the office until all hours. He hired a new associate named Julie and she is with him more than I am. I don't know how to handle it. I do everything I can to make Ted notice me and it doesn't work."

"Why don't you just ask him what is going on?" asked Stephanie.

"He is so moody. After the holidays, I promise I will find out what is going on."

Early in the afternoon, Sherry and Frankie arrived, and the four of them decided to plan a wives' get away in January.

Frankie suggested they go to her house in Vail. "It is so

beautiful in the winter, besides, when it's cold it's great to stay in by the fire and solve the problems of the world."

That suggestion sounded good to all of them so they called Ashley and she agreed.

"I really need to get away for a few days. How about January tenth to the fifteenth? My parents are coming for a couple of weeks so I know I can be gone for a few days."

"Great," said Frankie. I'll have the house opened, the refrigerator stocked and we're all set. We should probably meet at DIA in Denver and hire a limo for the trip up the mountain. Flying into the Eagle airport in the winter can be tricky."

Vicki immediately felt better. She had Christmas to plan for and then a trip to Vail to be with the wives.

The four couples had dinner at Frankie and Tom's beautiful home. Ted was cool, however, better than he had been on the plane.

In the hotel lobby, they said good night to Sherry, Bob, Stephanie and Joseph, and everyone went to their rooms.

Back in their room, Vicki put on her comfy T-shirt and boxer shorts and got into bed.

"What, no sexy negligee tonight?" asked Ted.

"Didn't think you were interested." replied Vicki.

"Well, have it your way." Ted said, turning his back to her.

The next day, the four wives went shopping on Union Square. Vicki didn't buy anything; she just wasn't in the mood. That evening, she and Ted dined alone at Tadich Grill. Ted's mood had definitely mellowed, but he kept checking his phone.

Finally, Vicki couldn't stand it and asked, "Ted, who are you waiting for?"

"Just some problems at the office. Julie said she would let me know what was going on"
In spite of the hurt, Vicki acted as if Julie wasn't important.

"Ted, the asbestos wives are going to get together in Vail, January-tenth. We are going to stay at Frankie's house. We think it would be good for Ashley." Vicki said.

"I wish you had talked to me first." Ted said. "I have to go to New York and I wanted you to go along; do what you want." "Sorry," replied Vicki.

Why does he have to make me feel guilty? Vicki asked herself.

The wives spent the last day in San Francisco making plane reservations so they would all arrive at DIA about the same time. They arranged for a limo to take them to Vail.

When Ted and Vicki boarded the firm's plane to fly home, Ted decided to ride in the cockpit with the pilot. Vicki tried to read, fell asleep and didn't wake until the plane landed.

Once they were back on the island, Vicki took Juno for a walk. Juno ran and chased critters and Vicki cried and wondered what had happened to her life. She was angry at herself, instead of being angry at Ted.

Vicki and Shirley talked the next day and Shirley said she wanted to have a black-tie party on December the tenth.

"Is that ok?" Shirley asked. "You don't have to do anything; I'm having it catered."

"Sounds perfect. How about spending a quiet Christmas on the island?" asked Vicki.

"Perfect, as long as you let me help with the food."

After their conversation, Vicki started looking around for Christmas decorations, but didn't find any. When Ted got home that night, she asked him if he had any decorations.

"Nope, never have a tree so don't need them."

He replied.

"Well, your parents and hopefully, your brother and family are going to be here for Christmas Day, so we need to decorate. I may invite Anna, Joe and the baby, too."

"As usual, you didn't ask me so I guess there is nothing I can do about it." Ted said.

"Ted, what is going on? Nothing I do is right," said Vicki with tears welling up in her eyes.

"Nothing is wrong, Vicki, you just seem to think it's okay to make plans and arrangements without talking to me about it."

"Oh, I didn't realize I had to get your approval for everything. If it's the money, I will go back to work and make my own spending money. I could even pay you rent." said Vicki more than a little irritated.

"See, you fly off the handle and say stupid things. There is no way I can talk to you. It's not the money. I've always had money and always will. It means nothing to me."

Vicki took Juno and walked out the door. After they walked about thirty-minutes, she dried her tears and tried to figure out what went wrong so fast with their brief marriage.

*You know it's Julie said the voice. She's an attorney, young* and impressionable."

Vicki and Juno went back to the cabin. Vicki noticed the Chris Craft was gone and thought to herself, good.

Vicki got busy and started making a list of decorations she needed for Christmas. She realized she couldn't begin to get them all in her Z4, and would need the Range Rover. She left a message on his voice mail.

"Ted, I'm going to need the Range Rover starting tomorrow. I can't begin to get Christmas decorations in my car."

Ted called right back, and said, "I'm sorry about this morning. Why don't you come to the mainland and we'll go to an early dinner?"

"That would be great." Vicki replied.

She showered and changed into a festive red sweater and jeans. She went out to the dock, boarded her boat and went to the mainland. At the last minute, she decided to take Juno, who loved the boat and the trip to the mainland.

She drove to Ted's office and she and Juno went in to say hello.

"Hi Sandy, is he in his office?" she asked.

"Hi Vicki, how's my favorite doggie? Yes, he is." Sandy answered.

Juno bounded up the stairs and went right to Ted's office. "Well, hello beautiful dog. What is your name?" asked a female voice.

"Hi Vicki, this is Julie, our new associate. Julie, meet my wife, Vicki and our spoiled dog-child Juno." laughed Ted.

"Hi Julie, welcome to the firm." replied Vicki.

She looks like a child thought Vicki, and, to think I've

been worried.

"Ted, I'm going to do some shopping. Do you mind if I trade cars?"

"Why don't I go with you? I'm through for the day."

"Great," said Vicki, smiling.

They left the office and decided to drop Juno off with the Martins while they shopped and went to dinner.

"We are going to get a very special early Christmas gift today." said Ted. "We both need an SUV, so you pick out the one you want and I'll put a big red bow on it."

"Oh Ted, that would be wonderful, but I don't want to give up my sports car."

"You don't have to give up the Beemer, it will be our summer fun-car." said Ted smiling.

"Oh Sweetie, I love you so much." said Vicki, smiling.

Vicki wanted a big SUV so they bypassed the BMW and Lexus dealers and went straight to the Cadillac dealer. Vicki found a black Escalade with a tan interior and all the buttons and whistles.

"Juno will love the back area. She can watch DVDs," laughed Vicki.

Ted wrote a check for the car and they left to go eat at their favorite Mexican restaurant, Los Arcos. After a satisfying dinner of tostados, sopaipillas and margaritas, they picked up Juno and went back to the Marina. They took both boats to the island.

Why is he so wonderful at times and then so horrible? Vicki asked herself, I'm always waiting for the other shoe to drop?

Once home, Ted went to his office to do some work and Vicki went to the bedroom. As she was preparing for bed, she noticed the phone line was busy. Just a client, she thought.

Then she did something she swore she would never do; she lifted the phone off its cradle, and carefully pressed the talk button.

"I'm sorry Babe," Ted was saying. "We had an argument this morning and I don't want to make her suspicious so I had to spend time with her."

Vicki put the phone back in its cradle with tears rolling down her cheeks. When Ted came up to bed, Vicki was pretending to be asleep. The next morning, she decided she needed some time away.

"Ted, I think I'll stay at the cottage for a couple of days so I can do all the shopping I need to do and I'll take Juno so you won't have to worry about her."

"Great idea," Ted said. "I know you will have this place standing tall for the holidays. Oh, the firm party is the fifteenth so please put that on your calendar and get yourself a pretty dress."

"I have a pretty dress, however, thanks for permission to buy another one," Vicki responded.

She went to the bedroom to pack a small bag. She had clothes at the cottage so didn't need much. She and Juno left in the boat before Ted left the house, and for some reason, that felt good. Let him stew for a while. I don't care she said to herself and immediately started crying.

When she got to the mainland and saw the Escalade, she felt a rage she had never felt before. Screw him, I'll spend so much of his money it will make his head spin, she said to herself. With Juno in the back, she drove to the cottage.

"George, could you follow me back to the marina so I can bring the Z4 home and put it in the garage?" she asked.

"Sure," replied George, looking at her with concern.

After they had both cars at the cottage, Vicki opened all the doors and windows, even though it was cold. She wanted fresh, clean air. Juno was busy running back and forth visiting all the places critters had been. Vicki watched her awhile and decided to try to forget about her problems. Then, she remembered Barb's advice.

"Barb, can we meet for lunch, I need a friend and advice?" asked Vicki.

"Sure honey, our usual place. I can take a longer lunch today since my judge is gone."

"Thanks, see you at eleven-thirty," replied Vicki.

Vicki found her list and added several more items to it, and went to her closet to change clothes. Hanging there was the olive-green Florida dress.

"I'll show you, you bastard." she said, smiling at the dress.

She stopped by the Martins and told them she would be gone for the afternoon and that Juno was outside.

"Don't worry, we'll watch our favorite four-legged friend." said Kathleen, looking worried.

Vicki thanked her and was glad neither Kathleen nor George asked her what was happening.

Vicki arrived at the restaurant before Barb, so she ordered a glass of wine and attempted to control her emotions.

Barb came, sat down and asked, "Oh no, what's happened?"

"I heard Ted and Julie on the phone last night and con-

77

firmed my suspicions that he is having an affair with her. I'm totally numb and also mad as hell. I am going to talk to a divorce attorney and I think I will also make an appointment with a psychologist. I need to stop being a doormat, first for my mom and now for Ted." Vicki said and she started crying.

"Oh, honey, I am so sorry, what can I do?"

"Just be my friend, Juno and I are staying at the cottage for a while, so just be around. I'm going to get through the holidays and then make permanent decisions. Oh, yes, he bought me a new Cadillac Escalade yesterday, and you know what else, I'm going to make sure he spends a lot more money on me."

"You go girl," exclaimed Barb.

"Why don't you come by for dinner after work?" asked Vicki. "I'm going to the store and will get something sinful for dinner."

"Sounds good to me, I'll be there about five-fifteen." said Barb.

Vicki spent the rest of the afternoon stocking the cottage and buying Christmas decorations. She decided she would get a tree for the cottage, so she bought decorations for that, too.

She returned to the cottage about three-thirty and decided to call.

"Hi Ashley, it's Vicki. How are you?"

"Hi Vic, so glad you called, I am feeling pretty low today."

"Well, this call won't help. I found out for sure that Ted is having an affair with Julie so I left and am at my little cottage. I don't know what to do next, I'm going to wait until after the holidays before I make permanent choices."

"Boy, our outing in January should be interesting!" exclaimed Ashley.

They talked for a few more minutes and then Vicki had to get ready for Barb.

There was a knock at her door. Please don't be Ted, she thought. She opened the door and it was Kathleen.

"Hi Sweetie, just wanted to see if you need anything?"

"Thanks, Kathleen, Juno and I are fine."

Barb arrived at five-fifteen, gave Juno a big hug and settled on the stool at the kitchen bar with a glass of wine. Vicki made pasta with meatballs, garlic bread, salad and chocolate sundaes for dinner.

"Barb, you are my lifeline. I really needed to laugh tonight and you are the talent. I hate to admit that I'm so much more relaxed here than I am on the island."

"That's a good thing, especially if you and Ted split." Barb replied.

Barb left at nine-thirty and Vicki went to the bedroom. She checked her cell and there was a call from Ted.

"Call me when you get this, I need to talk to you." he said.

Too bad, she thought as she turned off her phone and went to bed. She let Juno sleep on the bed with her and they both slept better than they had for some time.

Someone knocking on the door woke Vicki the next morning. She looked at the clock. It was seven.

"Vicki, let me in." said Ted, sounding irritated.

"Hi Ted, come on in. I'll make some coffee."

"Did you have company last night?" Ted asked looking at the dishes on the counter that Vicki hadn't washed the night before. "I guess you wasted no time finding another man to take care of you."

"Barb was here for dinner, if you must know, you're an asshole." cried Vicki.

She was so upset with herself because she was crying. "I'm not the one having an affair," she said loudly.

"I'm not having an affair; Julie is just a friend." Ted lied.

"What do you want Ted? I have things to do today."

"What are you doing here and why are you so upset? I told you Julie is just a friend."

"Ted, let's get through the holidays, since we have plans and talk about all of this after they are over."

"Okay, but you are being totally stupid." he said as he walked out the door, without waiting for a cup of coffee.

After he left, Vicki cleaned up the kitchen, showered and went shopping. Normally, she would never spend the amount of money she was spending, but somehow it made her feel like she had some control.

She ordered two large Christmas trees for the island and they would be delivered the following week. She hired a company to decorate the outside of the house and the island. She didn't care that they cost a fortune. She would show Ted who had class.

Later, she decided to go back to the island and get more clothes. She had a feeling that she wouldn't be living there again. She loaded the boat with some of her purchases and went to the island. She noticed the lake was starting to freeze and it wouldn't be too much longer until she could drive across the lake to the island.

When she approached the dock, she noticed the Chris Craft tied up. Hum wonder what I will find in the cabin.

She rang the doorbell to give Ted warning, just in case. When she walked into the cabin, he wasn't anywhere in sight. "Ted, are you here?"

"Up here," he answered.

She went up to his office and saw him sitting behind his desk with a glass of red wine. "Hi, when did you start drinking red wine?"

"It was open in the refrigerator so I decided to finish it off. What are you doing here?"

"I need a few more things and I wanted to bring some of the decorations over. What are you doing home?"

"I needed to get away from the office and do some serious thinking."
A feeling of dread came over Vicki and her eyes filled with tears.

"About?" she asked.

"Us, I have not been a good husband and I want things to change."

What? she thought.

They opened another bottle of wine and sat by the fire and talked for hours. Vicki called the Martins and asked them to take Juno for the night. After dinner, Vicki and Ted went to bed and made love for hours.

"Wow," Vicki said. "Maybe we should fight more often."

"I know, I have to tell you something. I had Julie here for

dinner one night while you were gone, and NO, we did not have sex."

"Thank you for telling me that. I have been worried. Could I ask that you use another associate for the asbestos cases? I can't handle you traveling with her when I don't go."

"In other words, you don't trust me."

"It's not that, it's my own insecurities."

"Let's talk about it later. Goodnight."

The next day Vicki felt like her life was back on track. She had renewed energy for the holidays. She went to the mainland to get Juno and put one of the cars in the garage at the marina. Then she did more Christmas shopping.

She went to the fly-fishing store and ordered a custom-made fly rod that Ted had been wanting. Good grief, two-thousand dollars for a fly rod, she thought. Oh well, it's only his money.

She and Ted went out for dinner and then took both boats back to the island. Juno looked a little confused. Huskies are always happy, so Juno just laid down and started snoring.

# 8

## The Holidays

Two huge Christmas trees were delivered to the island. Vicki supervised their placement, one by the fireplace and one on the deck overlooking the lake. Then she had the men decorate the outside of the house and some of the trees on the island. She was anxious for it to be dark so she could see how the trees looked with all the lights. She left the trees inside the cabin and on the deck for her and Ted to decorate.

She laid out all the lights and decorations by each tree and took inventory to see what else she would need. Two large wreaths were ready to be hung on the massive front doors.

Juno was enjoying smelling all the decorations and when Vicki showed her the husky ornaments, Juno acted like she understood they looked like her.

"Juno, maybe you need a partner for Christmas." She had been thinking about broaching the subject with Ted. Maybe tonight after wine and decorating.

Shirley called a few minutes later.

"How is the decorating going? I saw the delivery barge heading for the island this morning loaded with two big trees. I can't wait to see the cabin when you're finished. Ted has never decorated for Christmas."

"The trees are beautiful. I can't wait for tonight to see them with all the lights." Vicki replied.

"The open house has been scheduled for December 8th from seven to ten. It is black tie, so please make sure Ted wears his tux. Can't wait to see you in something wonderful." Shirley said.

"Oh, I have a dress that I bought in Key West and I hope it knocks Ted's socks off." laughed Vicki.

Vicki planned a simple dinner. Ted actually got home earlier than usual.

"WOW, the dock and trees look wonderful. Maybe we should put a small tree on the dock to greet people when they arrive. I thought we could have a party here for the firm since you are going to all this work. Is that ok?" he asked.

Vicki was thrilled he was pleased and wanted to show off what she had planned.

"Of course, it's ok." she replied.

After dinner, they started decorating the first tree. Ted was in a good mood and kept Vicki laughing with his teasing. Juno joined in by howling. When the first tree was finished, they stepped back and turned on the lights. Ted stood behind Vicki and put his arms around her waist.

"You know I love you." he whispered in her ear.

Vicki's mood soared; life was wonderful. *The voice started to speak ... Shut Up! Vicki screamed back!* When they went to bed later that night, they snuggled and Vicki felt her life was perfect.

The next morning after Ted left for the office, Vicki dressed and decided to go to the mainland for more decorations for the house and invitations for the party. She called Barb to see if she wanted to do lunch.

"How about an early Christmas lunch?"

"Sure, let's go someplace special. How about The Bar at the lodge?"

"Sounds good to me, see you at eleven-thirty."

Vicki quickly dressed and took the boat to the mainland. Once there, she did some quick shopping and drove to the lodge to meet Barb. As she walked into The Bar, she abruptly stopped and stared at Ted and Julie sitting in a booth. She was about to storm over and confront them, when two other attorneys from the firm joined them. Vicki walked over.

"Hi Sweetie, what a pleasant surprise. Can you join us? We're having an informal meeting. You are more than welcome to stay." said Ted, rising and kissing Vicki on the cheek.

"Thanks, Barb and I wanted to eat someplace nicer than The Verdict. See you after work Ted, bye."

As she and Barb sat down, Barb gave Vicki a questioning look.

"So, what is that about?" she asked.

"Some kind of meeting," replied Vicki.

They had a couple of glasses of wine and talked about the upcoming holidays.

"Ted's parents are having a fancy catered party this weekend. I need to see if their caterer can do our party on the fifteenth. You are available that night, aren't you?"

"Of course, who will be there?"

"Mostly the firm, that's why I want you there. I need someone to talk to about something other than law." replied Vicki.

After lunch, Vicki did more shopping, went to the cottage to get her dress for Saturday night, then to the marina, and home. The lake was almost frozen and Harvey kept a channel clear for the boats, until the ice was thick enough to drive on.

Life was mellow the rest of the week in the Winter household. When Vicki walked down the stairs in the olive-green cocktail dress the night of Ted's parents' party, he whistled and a broad smile crossed his face.

"Wow, you look sensational, maybe we'll stay home." he said in a husky voice.

"Thank you, Sweetheart, you make me feel beautiful. You look quite handsome yourself. We do make a good-looking couple."

She thought, we would have beautiful babies, and then thought better not to say it.

They had the hardtop on the Cris Craft and the heater on as they crossed the lake. Once on the other side, they drove to Ted's parents' home where a valet parked the Range Rover.

"Look at all the people and the fancy cars. Your parents must know everyone who is anyone."

"I think they do. Look there's the governor, a senator, a movie producer and a possible candidate for the presidency. They do move in interesting circles."

As they entered the large living area all eyes turned toward them. Vicki was sure all talking stopped. All at once, everyone started clapping. Vicki was embarrassed, until she turned around looked into the eyes of the Vice President of the United States.

"Oh, I am so sorry Sir. You should be in front of us."

"Of course not, my dear, everyone is staring at Ted's beautiful wife. Hello Ted, how are you?" asked the VP.

"Very well Sir. I would like to introduce my wife, Vicki."

After the introductions, Vicki went to say hello to Shirley.

"Shirley, this is an amazing party. I sent out the invitations for our party and I am hoping your caterers are available. You look amazing."

"Oh honey, you took everyone's breath away. Ted certainly made the best decision of his life when he married you. We will talk with the caterer before the night is over."

The party went to the wee hours of the morning. Vicki made arrangements with the caterer for their party.

Ted and Vicki went back to the marina. Harvey came out and said they could drive across the lake; he had plowed a trail for the cars. Then, he handed Vicki a wiggling bundle.

"Mr. Winter wanted me to give you this guy tonight. Merry Christmas Mrs. Winter," said Harvey.

She looked at the head popping out of the blanket. Blue husky puppy eyes stared up at her.

"Oh, she-he is beautiful, thank you darling."

"Well, I know you wanted another husky for Juno, so this is Sitka, also a rescue and she's a little girl." smiled Ted.

When they got to the cabin, Vicki introduced Sitka to Juno. She sat and watched them until she was sure things were okay. She let the dogs out and went with them to make sure Sitka would stay with Juno. Juno brought Sitka back to the door looking like a proud mother. When Vicki went up to bed, she looked over the railing and smiled at her dogs curled up together in Juno's bed.

She kissed Ted and thanked him for getting Sitka. "You are so wonderful."

"You deserve the best." he replied and they went to sleep wrapped in each other's arms.

The next week was a whirlwind of activity getting ready for the party. The decorators completed their work and the island looked like a winter wonderland. The caterers came early the day of the party to set up and start preparing food. The weather was warmer than usual so there were tables outside with heaters, and the outside fireplace was burning. Blankets were available for people who wanted to be outside. The inside of the house was festive and Vicki was very proud of it.

Ted got dressed in a red shirt, jeans, and blazer and looked quite handsome. Vicki wore a red V-neck sweater, black jeans and boots. The V-neck showed cleavage and her olive skin. She had her hair in a ponytail and she felt great. Juno and Sitka also wore red collars. They had bonded quickly and were always together.

The party was a success and everyone enjoyed themselves. Vicki had not seen Judge Gresham for months, so they had a long talk catching up.

"You look wonderful and happy. I think I was wrong about Ted before you got married." said Judge Gresham.

"Thank you, Bob. We've had some bumps but I think things have finally settled down." replied Vicki, crossing her fingers.

Vicki spent some time with Julie and learned she had a

long-distance relationship and her fiancé was due in Stone Mountain tomorrow.

"When are you getting married?" asked Vicki.

"No date set yet and I'm beginning to wonder if we should, so I'll be glad to spend some time with Matt."

"You'll work it out. What does Matt do?"

"He's a prosecutor in Denver."

At that point, Ted came up behind Vicki, put his arms around her waist and kissed her neck.

Vicki blushed as she felt like she had won a long battle.

See Julie, he is mine, she thought.

"Hello you sexy, gorgeous woman." Ted teased.

"Hi Honey, Julie was telling me about her fiancé. He will be here tomorrow. Perhaps the four of us can do dinner while he is here. "

"Sounds great," replied Ted.

Julie seemed reluctant to commit, "I'll let you know after we see what our plans are."

The party broke up shortly after and the caterers cleaned up. Ted and Vicki took wine and went out on the deck. The full moon shining on the lake was beautiful and Vicki felt totally at peace. Juno and Sitka were curled up together with husky smiles on their faces.

Life really is wonderful, thought Vicki.

Ted was home more than usual the next few days and he helped get ready for Christmas Day on the island. In addition to Ted's parents, his brother and family, Anna and her family would be there. There were many presents under the tree for Bonnie and several boxes for Vicki. Vicki was hiding Ted's present since a fly rod was difficult to wrap.

"I guess Santa doesn't like me, I don't see any gifts for me under the tree."

"Oh, just you wait. You're like a little boy." laughed Vicki.

Anna, Joe and baby Bonnie arrived the next day. Bonnie had started walking and talking a mile a minute. At first Juno and Sitka watched her, turning their heads from side to side trying to figure out what this little person was all about. It took only a few minutes before Bonnie and the two dogs were chasing each other and the house was full of baby squeals, husky howls and adult laughter. This is what Christmas was all about.

I really want a baby of my own, thought Vicki. I'll bring the topic up after the holidays are over. Ted seems to be happy so maybe he's ready.

After dinner, Anna put Bonnie to bed and the two dogs laid down beside the crib and were snoring away within minutes. Anna came back downstairs and the four adults sat by the fire. Vicki offered everyone wine which Anna refused.

"What, no wine?" asked Vicki raising an eyebrow.

"No, not in my condition," replied Anna. "It's not good for the baby."

"Oh Anna, I am so happy for you," exclaimed Vicki, feeling a little envious.

"Well done old man." replied Ted looking at Joe.

The next day was Christmas Eve. Anna and Vicki went

to town to do last minute shopping and to buy provisions for Christmas dinner.

"You and Ted seem happy." commented Anna.

"We've had some rough patches; things are great now." Vicki replied, once again crossing her fingers.

That night they cooked a traditional Italian dinner. They all ate and drank too much. Everyone felt relaxed.

At six a.m. the next morning there was much squealing, barking and howling.

"What?" asked Ted.

"It's Christmas morning and we have a little one in the house. This is perfect." smiled Vicki.

With coffee in hand, the adults sat by the tree as Bonnie tore into her many packages. Juno and Sitka smelled their presents and tore the paper off to get to the treats. Then, they helped Bonnie open some of her gifts. About twenty-minutes later Bonnie was playing with the boxes that the gifts had been in and the dogs were eating their breakfast, so the adults could open their gifts.

Ted gave Vicki a small, oblong box. Inside was a beautiful diamond bracelet.

"Oh Ted, it's beautiful. The Escalade and Sitka were enough." Vicki said with tears in her eyes.

"You had to have something under the tree," Ted replied. "Oh look, here's another gift with your name on it." Inside the box were diamond earrings.

Vicki exclaimed, "Thank you, they are beautiful."

Anna and Joe opened the gifts from Ted and Vicki.

Anna loved the cashmere sweater and Joe was happy with a Harris Tweed sports jacket.

"There will be another gift delivered to your house next week." Vicki said. She and Ted had sent them a painting they found at a gallery and immediately knew it was for Joe and Anna.

Finally, Ted was sitting among several gifts from Joe, Anna and Bonnie. There were two boxes from Vicki. Ted opened the gifts and thanked everyone for them.

"Hum, something seems to be missing." said Vicki as she left the room.

She came back with a long, round tube wrapped in paper with a fly-fishing theme.

When Ted opened the tube, and saw the fly rod, he looked up at Vicki with pure love in his eyes.
"Oh, it is just what I wanted. Thank you so much,"
he said.

"I know, Jimmy at the fly shop helped me."

Henry and Shirley arrived late morning and more gifts were opened as mimosas were served. Bonnie and the dogs were busy tearing up wrapping paper, playing with gift boxes and ignoring the actual gifts.

Shirley, Anna and Vicki went to the kitchen to start preparing the holiday feast. Vicki had been baking and preparing food for weeks and Shirley was so impressed.

"I must say, my son struck gold when he met you. Thank you for teaching him to be a more caring person." Shirley remarked.

Vicki thought, that was a strange thing for Shirley to say about her son, and then dismissed the thought.

Anna put Bonnie down for a nap, and both dogs immediately laid down by her crib, all three were soon sound asleep.

Vicki and Anna picked up all the torn paper and boxes. Vicki was imagining what it would be like to have a child of her own.

Finally, the prime rib was cooked and every one sat down to dine. The conversation was lively and the food was perfect. Vicki was remembering holidays with Jack's family. She didn't think any holiday could be better, but this holiday was perfection.

After dessert, Henry and Shirley left. Sam, Anna and Bonnie went to bed early. Ted and Vicki sat in front of the fire, holding hands.

"This was perfect," said Vicki.

"You made it perfect," replied Ted.

Vicki was happy as they went up to bed where they made love, falling asleep in each other's arms.

Life is perfect, thought Vicki.

Sam, Anna and Bonnie left on December twenty-seventh. The Winter household settled into the lull between Christmas and New Year's. Julie called and invited them to a small gathering on New Year's Eve so they could meet Matt.

"We would love to meet Matt so what can we bring?" asked Vicki.

"Just yourselves; Ted has the address."

Vicki wore a black jumpsuit to the party and knew she looked good.

"Honey, you look amazing." said Ted.

"Thank you. You look pretty inviting yourself." laughed Vicki.

When they met Matt, Vicki immediately liked him although she felt a certain tension in the room. Julie was a gracious hostess except that Vicki noticed she paid way too much attention to Ted so Vicki mentioned it to him on the way home.

"Oh, you are such an insecure little girl." Ted said showing irritation.

Damn, here we go again, Vicki thought.

New Year's Day was very quiet. Vicki slept late and then spent the rest of the day taking decorations off the trees. She tried to keep busy as she felt depressed and very tired. Ted spent most of the day in his office.

## 9

# The New Year

The week after the holidays was busy for Vicki. She got the house back to normal and started planning for the wives' long weekend in Vail.

Ted was busy at work, working long hours. He was off to New York City to speak at a medical conference on the effects of asbestos on the body. Vicki felt guilty not being able to go with him although he hadn't told her about his New York trip until she told him about Vail.

One evening Ted seemed quite tense. He walked in the door, went right to the bar and poured a glass of scotch.

"Bad day?" asked Vicki.

"It was ok, I'm just buried with the conference and trying to keep all the balls in the air with the cases. Thank goodness Julie is going with me. She can keep things running smoothly while I'm busy." Ted said.

"I didn't realize you were taking her to New York." said Vicki, feeling a sense of panic.

"Don't start. She needs to get away since she and Matt

split." Ted said, starting to sound irritated.

"You don't think I have a right to be concerned? You're upset with me because I'm going to Vail and not to New York with you, and then you take a young, attractive woman who just broke up with her fiancé."

"Obviously, you still don't trust me." Ted replied in a monotone.

"Oh, never mind. You obviously don't care about my feelings. I guess I should feel honored that you told me." said Vicki with tears in her eyes.

There was definitely a chill in the air between Ted and Vicki during the time before they both left, Vicki going to Vail, Ted off to New York.

The day before Vicki was leaving for Vail, she decided to go to the cottage and take the shuttle to the airport. She put Juno, Sitka and her luggage in the Escalade and drove across the lake. She called Barb to invite her to the cottage for dinner. As she was driving toward the mainland, she spotted Ted's Range Rover heading toward the island.

"Where are you going?" asked Ted.

"I'm taking the dogs to the Martin's and staying at the cottage tonight. I'll take the shuttle to the airport tomorrow."

"I thought we would go out for dinner tonight. I was going to suggest that you fly with me in the firm's jet, to Denver on my way to New York."

"Oh, so now you want to be nice, well, no thank you." replied Vicki, very irritated.

She raised her window and drove off before he could reply.

Once Vicki got to the cottage, she calmed down. The

Martins were immediately in love with Sitka. Juno was showing Sitka around the cottage grounds. George and Kathleen were laughing at the two dogs. Vicki felt so much better being back at the cottage and with the Martins.

"Vicki, I would be more than happy to take you to the airport tomorrow if Ted can't." offered George.

"Thank you, I don't want to burden you, however, I would appreciate the ride."

After George, Kathleen and the dogs left for their house, Vicki went to the cottage. She always felt good being there. After work, Barb arrived and they enjoyed pizza and beers in front of the fireplace.

"Is everything ok?" asked Barb.

"Could be better. I'm not going to burden you with the details."

The next morning Vicki dressed in warm clothes and called George to let him know she was ready to leave.

"Do you want me to wait with you inside?" asked George.

"Thank you, George, I will be fine. You are so kind to give me a ride." Vicki replied as she hugged him.

"You know, Kathleen and I think of you as the daughter we never had."

"You're going to make me cry." said Vicki trying to hold back the tears.

Once on the plane, Vicki settled in her seat and started reading her Kindle.

She thought to herself, it is so nice flying first class. *Really though, is it worth it to be treated like dirt, the voice in her head asked?*

I can't think about it right now, so go away, she thought

to herself.

Once she landed in Denver, her mood had definitely improved. Why do I always feel relieved when I'm away from Ted? she asked herself.

When she went to the baggage claim area, she immediately spotted the other wives. After many hugs and kisses, they headed to ground transportation to find their limo for the ride up I-70 to Vail.

Once inside the limo, champagne was poured and they toasted to each other.

"Ashley, you look stunning. Being single definitely agrees with you." said Sherry.

"You have no idea. I no longer have to worry about who Jason is sleeping with. I heard through the grapevine that he and Charlotte are having problems. It does my heart good." replied Ashley.

"Aren't you a little sad? How are the girls doing?" asked Vicki.

"Sure, I get sad and remember the good times, BM." said Ashley.

"WHAT?" the others asked in unison.

"BM means, before money," answered Ashley.

Wanting to elaborate, Ashley continued, "Money can really screw things up. It's nice to have an opulent lifestyle, although, when it becomes the most important thing in your life, it's just not worth it. Of course, I'm fortunate that I don't have to work though I know I could. The girls are very angry with us, but they will survive."

It was a clear Colorado day with blue sky and puffy white clouds. The wives became silent as the limo started up Floyd Hill.

"I miss Colorado," said Vicki. "It will always be home to me. I know I will be back someday."

"It is beautiful," replied Frankie.

They finally arrived at Frankie's Colorado house. It was beautiful with a view of Vail Valley and Gore Creek.

Once they had settled in, wine was served and they began to catch up with their lives.

"Wow, this is so different than La Jolla. I love the snow." Sherry exclaimed. "Life is much the same. Robert works and I invest my trust money. If he only knew how much money I have, he would probably quit working. No, he wouldn't, his ego is too big. He loves being the center of attention. We will grow old together and maybe someday find we do have a deep love, who knows."

Stephanie was watching the girls and finally her gaze stopped on Vicki. "Vicki, honey, are you ok?" asked Stephanie.

"Once again, things are a little rough right now. The holidays were wonderful so I'm trying to convince myself it's just post-holiday blues. How are you and Joe?"

"Oh, we are just an old married couple who are comfortable. It actually feels good. I still want you all in Florida in March for the anniversary party."

"We'll be there," replied four voices in unison as a van pulled into the driveway.

"Here's dinner; I ordered Italian to be delivered so we wouldn't have to cook or go out tonight." said Frankie.

They sat around a huge table with an antler chandelier hanging over it. There was a fireplace in one end of the dining room and floor-to-ceiling windows in the other end looking out on the forest. There was fresh snow on the spruce trees and the full moon made it look like a fairy land.

After dinner, they changed into warm pajamas and sat on the floor by the fireplace in the great room.

Finally, Vicki felt she had to be truthful.

"As I said, the holidays were wonderful except these past ten days that have been pure hell. Maybe it's me. I am so tired all the time, and Ted has gone back to shutting me out and being angry for no reason. He is in New York City right now with Julie his associate who dumped her fiancé over the holidays. Am I wrong for being worried?"

"No way. I was always worried about Jason because I knew what he was like before we started dating. It's strange, you always think you are the only one and they will change however, they usually don't." said Ashley.

"I just don't understand," said Vicki. "They pursue us and won't take "no" for an answer. Finally, we fall in love and give our hearts to them and what do they do? They want us when they want us, they make us feel like everything is our fault and yet, we put up with it."

Wow, where did that come from? thought Vicki. I'm tired of it, I don't deserve to be treated this way. Things are going to change once I get home.

That night when Vicki went to bed, she turned her cell phone off and went to sleep. The next morning, she woke and didn't feel well. She went to the bathroom and was sick. Must have been something I ate, she thought, I hope the others aren't ill.

As they all sat around the table drinking coffee, Stephanie asked: "Vicki, honey, are you ok? You are very pale."

"Something I ate last night did not agree with me."

"Well, we can just hang out here today," said Frankie.

"No, you guys go do something. I will be okay." replied Vicki.

After the others left for Vail Village, Vicki went back to her room and fell asleep, not even thinking about her cell phone.

When the others returned, they brought Vicki flowers and a gorgeous martini glass from The Golden Bear. As they made drinks or poured themselves a glass of wine, Vicki declined and drank water from her new glass.

"What shall we do for dinner?" asked Sherry.

"What do you feel like Vicki?" Frankie wanted to know. "I know Sweet Basil always has good food and homemade soup, or Up the Creek probably has something that would be easy on your tummy."

"I am so sorry, you guys. I may have been exposed to the flu before I left. Sure, hope none of you get it. I am feeling better so let's go to Sweet Basil. It has always been my favorite."

At the restaurant, Vicki ordered soup and a cup of hot tea. She felt much better. When they returned to the house, Vicki realized she had left her cell phone in her room. She got the phone, turned it on and had a message from Ted.

"Hi Vic, just wanted to say 'hi' and tell you I miss you. If you try to call and I don't answer, don't worry. I'm buried in work and may not hear the phone. I'm in room seventeen-twenty." Vicki called the hotel and asked for room seventeen-twenty.

"Hello," Julie answered.

Vicki immediately hung up.

Why did I call him? she asked herself.

Her cell phone rang and caller ID said it was Ted. "Hi," she answered.

"Did you just try to call?" asked Ted. "Julie and I are finishing up some work in my room."

"Why did she answer your cell phone?"

"What is the big deal? She was sitting closer to it than me." Ted answered, irritated.

"Just wanted to say 'hi'," Vicki said.

"I'll talk to you later."

"Ok, you have a good night." And, he hung up.

Damn, why do I let him to this to me? And, what is *she* doing in his room thought Vicki, going to sleep with tears?

The next day Vicki felt much better so the wives decided to rent snow shoes and go hiking.

"Wow, this is really hard work." said Sherry.

"I know, it feels good to be outside in the cold again." said Vicki.

Later, the wives went to Up the Creek for lunch. They all ordered the turkey and brie sandwiches, French fries and wine. "Oh, I am so full and the sandwich was so good." said Vicki.

Everyone agreed that lunch was great. They decided to buy groceries and cook at the house that night.

After dinner, the wives put on warm clothes and took a walk in the snow. The moon was still bright and almost full and the air was cold and crisp. When they returned, they had hot chocolate by the fire and went to bed.

When Vicki went to her room and checked her phone, there was a text from Ted.

It read: "Shutting phone off for the night. Will call to-morrow. Love you."

Screw him, thought Vicki and she went to sleep. Once again, she didn't feel well the next morning.

"Vicki, are you pregnant?" asked Stephanie.

"Heavens no," replied Vicki, and then she started thinking about the possibility.

To take her mind off the possibility of being pregnant and Ted sleeping with Julie, Vicki started thinking about what the wives could do to help asbestos victims and their families.

The next morning, Vicki suggested they start thinking about it.

"You know guys, I still want to do something good for the families of asbestos victims. We are all living the good life as a result of their suffering. I really think we should try to help them."

Ashley replied, "You know, I've been thinking about it, too. Since I don't have a husband to keep happy, why don't I talk to an attorney and see what we need to do to get started?"

They all agreed that was a good idea.

The rest of the time in Vail was spent relaxing and tossing around ideas for a foundation.

When the wives parted at DIA in Denver, Vicki had a feeling of dread. She was still not feeling well in the mornings and she knew the situation with Ted had to be resolved.

# 10

## Big Surprises Come in Small Packages

When Vicki's plane landed, George was waiting with Juno and Sitka. Both huskies were howling their greetings which made Vicki smile.

"Hi George, thank you for picking me up. Hello my ladies. I know George and Kathleen spoiled you rotten."

"They are so glad their human is home."

I wish Ted felt the same, and I wish I felt glad to be going to the island, thought Vicki.

Once they arrived at the cottage, Vicki decided to stay there for the night because she needed some time to herself.

After she closed the door, she started crying for no reason. Both dogs came up and put their heads on her knees. She hugged them both and sobbed in their soft fur.

Once she stopped crying, she looked in the refrigerator for something to eat and found Kathleen had cooked lasagna for her. She heated it up and thought about having a glass of wine, then she decided to drink water instead.

She called Ted and left a message that she was going to spend the night at the cottage because she was so tired. His phone went right to voicemail so she was relieved.

After she ate dinner, she went to bed and started thinking about the foundation she wanted to start. Hopefully, the others would want to help. If they didn't, she would find a way to do it herself.

Vicki woke up the next morning very sick to her stomach. After she was feeling a little better, she decided she needed to see the doctor. If, and it was a big if, she was pregnant, she would have to do whatever was necessary since she was a Rh baby, born with eleven Rh negative factors. Then there would be the problem of telling Ted.

Should I plan a romantic dinner? Should I just come out and tell him when we are alone and he was in a good mood? she asked herself.

At nine a.m. she phoned Dr. Peterson's office and scheduled an appointment.

"Hi Audrey, it's Vicki Winter and I need to see Dr. Peterson. I may be pregnant, and I was an Rh baby." said Vicki.

"Vicki, come in at ten-thirty, we just had a cancellation."

Vicki took a shower, washed her hair and as she was drying off, the phone rang.

"Hello."

"Hi Vic, sorry you stayed at the cottage last night. I missed you and the girls." Ted said.

"I wasn't feeling well and I was very tired and had an upset stomach, so I stayed here."

"When will you be home?"

"Before you get home from work. See you then," she said.

She dressed, fed the dogs, told Kathleen she had an errand and would be gone till about noon.

"Oh, and thank you for the lasagna. It was so good." she said to Kathleen.

"You're welcome dear. We'll take care of the girls while you are gone."

Vicki drove to town and found a parking space close to Dr. Peterson's office. Ted's office was in the next block, although she had no desire to see her husband right then. Maybe after her appointment she would see if he wanted to go to lunch.

"Vicki, what are your symptoms?" asked Dr. Peterson.

"I am exhausted all the time; I get sick most mornings and I feel strange. If I could be pregnant, you need to know I was an Rh-negative baby, eleven factors."

After a blood test and a urine sample, Dr. Peterson said, "We will have the results tomorrow, however, from my exam, I suspect you are pregnant."

When Vicki heard this, she burst into tears. She knew her world was about to change and she didn't know how. "Are you emotional most of the time?" asked Dr. Peterson.

"Lately, I sure am. What do I do if I am pregnant, to make sure the baby is ok?"

"The blood work will show if you are pregnant and if you are, we will send you to an OBGYN who specializes in difficult pregnancies. There is much that can be done."

After Vicki left the office, she went back to the cottage. She was sound asleep when her phone rang. She looked at the clock, it was five p.m. She should have been back on the island.

"Hello," she answered.

"Hey, why aren't you here? I thought you were coming home today." said Ted.

"I have a bad case of the flu. I saw Dr. Peterson today and he said bed rest for a day or two so I thought I would stay at the cottage and not expose you."

"OK, can I bring you anything?" he asked.

"No thanks," she replied and hung up.

The next day, she waited by the phone for Dr. Peterson's call.

This is like being a teenager waiting for *him* to call, she thought.

Finally, at ten a.m. the phone rang.

"Vicki, Dr. Peterson would like you to come back in today. Can you be here in thirty-minutes?" asked Audrey.

"I'll be there," said Vicki with a feeling of dread coming over her.

Once she was in the examining room, Dr. Peterson came in, followed by a very distinguished looking man.

"Good morning Vicki, this is Dr. Carter. I told you about him yesterday." said Dr. Peterson.

"Hi, so I guess this means I am pregnant?"
asked Vicki.

"The test isn't totally conclusive although I'm pretty sure you are."

Taking the lead, Dr. Carter asked, "Vicki, since it is pretty sure you are pregnant, Dr. Peterson wanted me involved immediately. We will do another test today, one that is more detailed and see what it tells us. The antibody test won't tell us much right now. If you are sensitized, we'll give you an Immunoglobulin (Rhlg) shot and it will help. If you are pregnant, is this your first pregnancy? Even if you miscarried or had an ectopic pregnancy, I need to know."

"This will be my first. I swore I would never get pregnant because my mother was physically and psychologically abusive and I didn't want to do that to a child."

"Well, just because your mom was abusive doesn't mean you will be." said Dr. Peterson.

"Hope not because it sounds like I'm going to be a mom."

Dr. Peterson said they put a rush on the tests.

When Vicki got back to the cottage, she was calm and excited. She was going to be a mom.

"You will never know the fear I knew as a child." she told her tummy.

The dogs were subdued, as if they knew something was different.

"Hi Barb, wanted to call and tell you I'm home."

"How was your weekend? You sound different somehow. Is everything ok?".

"I don't know. Could you come over after work?"

"See you then. Wine?"

"Nope, not drinking,"

Vicki spent the day thinking about a baby. Her emotions swung between happiness and fright.

Barb arrived after work. They had left over lasagna for dinner. Then they lit a fire, sat and talked. Barb was excited for Vicki when she learned of the possible pregnancy.

"How will Ted take the news if it is positive?" she asked Vicki.

"Don't know and don't care. I would hope he would be happy and excited. He has said he didn't want children, so I could travel with him. Of course, that was before Julie. It doesn't really matter. If I am pregnant, he will be a dad and will have to accept the baby."

After Barb left, Vicki went to bed and slept well. The next morning, she felt much better. Dr. Carter called and said she was pregnant and she was sensitized so he would become her primary doctor.

"Don't worry, enjoy your pregnancy. We will make sure you deliver a healthy baby." he assured her.

"Thank you, Dr. Carter, what do we do now?"

"I will need to see you weekly until your second trimester. How about we set a schedule now?"

"Sounds good, anytime is fine for me. I live on the island so it will take a little longer for me to get to the appointments."

"No problem, if we do run into problems, is there someplace you can stay that's closer to the hospital?"

"I keep a cottage at the Martins, so that's no problem."

"Okay, I'll transfer you to Monica. She will set up a weekly appointment."

After the appointments were scheduled, Vicki decided it was time to deal with telling Ted. She would see if he could go to lunch thinking that if they were in a restaurant, she hoped that he wouldn't get openly angry.

"Hi Sandy, is Ted in?" asked Vicki.

"Sure, I'll transfer you."

"Hi Vic, are you feeling better? I miss you."

"Much better, thanks. I'm hungry, how about lunch today?"

"Sounds great, come by about eleven-thirty."

"Okay, see you then."

She hoped she wasn't making a mistake. Vicki showered and took extra time with her hair and makeup. She wore black jeans, a black V-neck sweater, black riding boots and a black leather bomber jacket.

Smiling at the huskies she said, "Wish me luck girls, I'm going to lunch with your daddy. Hopefully, we can go home to the island today."

She walked up the stairs to Ted's office, opened the door and stopped in her tracks; Julie was standing behind Ted's chair massaging his neck.

"Oh, hi hon," he said, obviously embarrassed.

"Hi Vicki, how was Vail?" asked Julie.

"Ted, are we still going to lunch?" asked Vicki, obviously ignoring Julie.

"Sure, let me close this file and we're off."

"Ted, don't forget our meeting this afternoon at one-thirty," Julie said, smiling at Vicki.

"I'll be back, if not, start without me."

# 11

## Crisis

They arrived at the restaurant and settled into a booth. As they were looking at the menu, Vicki told Ted she was pregnant.

"I told you before we got married, I don't want kids!'" shouted Ted.

Feeling a sense of panic, Vicki cried and said, "Why not? We can definitely afford a baby. The island would be a great place to raise a child and I'm not working, so I can be home."

"Well, if you want to keep this marriage alive, you will have an abortion and have it soon." yelled Ted as he stormed out of the restaurant.

Back at the cottage, Vicki broke down in tears. She needed to talk to someone, so she called Anna.

"Hi Vicki, I was just about to call you. Sam and I are having twins."

"Oh Anna, I'm happy for you. I need to talk. I'm also

pregnant and Ted told me I have to get rid of it immediately."

"Vicki, I am so sorry. I'm sure he will change his mind. When he has a chance to think about it and settle down, he will realize the baby has his genes and his ego won't let him not want it."

"I sure hope so because I'm not going to get rid of this child. It's almost like I have a chance to make up for mother. Look at you, you are a great mom and would never do anything to hurt your children."

They talked for an hour and when they hung up, Vicki felt better and believed Ted would come around.

She went to bed and slept well, with Juno and Sitka on the bed with her. The next morning, she wasn't sick. That hadn't happened for over a week. Vicki felt excited about the baby and wanted to talk to Ted. She called his cell and it went to voicemail. At nine she called the office and Sandy told her that Ted was out for a couple of days.

"Is Julie there?" asked Vicki.

"Haven't heard from her. Do you want me to have her call you?" replied Sandy.

"No thanks" said Vicki, hanging up.

Next, she called Barb and invited her to lunch. She needed to talk to someone who was on her side.

"Hi Sweetie," said Barb as she sat down. "You look totally lost, what can I do?"

"Just be my friend and I need you desperately right now. I am pregnant, and Ted is insisting I have an abortion."

"What a jerk. You would think he would want a child to carry the name. He will come around." Barb said, taking Vicki's hand.

They had their lunch and then Barb had to go back to work. Vicki decided to go by Ted's office to see if his car was there. It wasn't. Then, she decided to drive by Julie's apartment. As she was approaching the building, she noticed Ted and Julie walking down the street holding hands.

"So, there is nothing going on?" she screamed as she pulled in front of them.

"Vicki, you don't understand" said Julie with a gleam in her eye.

"Shut Up, you home wrecker!" yelled Vicki.

"Vicki, don't talk to Julie like that. You don't understand what I need and right now it isn't a child."

"So, every time something happens that doesn't fit into your life, you go running to your whore!" screamed Vicki. "Don't think I'll just let this pass. You are going to be a father and you will pay for it for the next twenty years. I am not getting rid of our child."

"She's pregnant?" Julie asked, backing away from Ted.

"Yes, she obviously did it on purpose." Replied Ted.

Vicki had no response. She drove off, tears running down her cheeks. She went to the island, packed most of her clothes and put her belongings and the dogs in the Escalade and drove to the cottage.

Vicki spent several days by herself, not wanting to see or talk to anyone, including the Martin's. She cried until there were no tears left.

Thoughts flooded her brain in the form of unanswered questions.

What should I do? How can I afford to support myself

and a child? I'm still young enough to work and surely, I'll get some kind of support from Ted. I have to find an attorney who is willing to go against Ted.

She immediately started searching for an attorney in other towns near Stone Mountain. She called several and was told they would get back to her; fat chance of that happening.

One morning her phone rang quite early.

"Is this Vicki Winter?" asked the male voice.

"Yes, it is, who is calling?"

"My name is Gary Livingston and I understand you are looking for a divorce attorney who is willing to take on Ted Winter. I would be interested in taking your case."

"Isn't it unethical for you to contact me and solicit my case?"

"We don't have to tell anyone I called you."

"If I remember right, Ted beat you badly in a big case. Are you out for revenge?"

"Of course not, although, I would like to see the finances of Ted's firm."

"No thanks. I'll do you a favor and not tell anyone you called me, if you promise to never call again."

Gary hung up and Vicki felt a strange sense of power. "Hum, I *can* take control of my life."

She had a doctor's appointment. She showered, and when she looked in the mirror, she was shocked at how gaunt she looked. She said goodbye to the girls and left for town.

As she stopped at a light, Ted pulled up beside her.

"Hey, I need to talk to you NOW."

"I have an appointment and don't want to talk to you. As far as I'm concerned, you have made your feelings known and I'm not going to do what you want. See you later."

She drove to her appointment, feeling better all the way, remembering the look on Ted's face. As she was parking, her phone rang.

"Vicki darling, it's Shirley. What is happening? Ted said you guys were having some serious problems and you moved out."

"Shirley, I don't have time to talk right now. I have an appointment. I'll call later."

When Dr. Carter walked into the examining room, he was shocked at Vicki's appearance. "Vicki what is going on? Are you eating?"

"Dr. Carter, Ted is insisting I get an abortion so we are now separated."

"Well, you sure don't need that right now. Do you want an abortion?"

"Never, I want this child."

After Dr. Carter examined Vicki and took blood, he wrote a prescription for prenatal vitamins and told Vicki she needed bed rest immediately.

"At your appointment next week, we will do an ultrasound and see what we can see. Right now, I want you home in bed."

Vicki drove to the cottage and Kathleen was waiting for her. "Sweetie, what is going on?"

"Oh Kathleen, I'm pregnant, Ted doesn't want it and my doctor just put me on bed rest for a week. I don't know what to do."

"Don't you worry about a thing. You make a list of what you need from the store and I'll send George. I'll cook some things you can freeze. You go sit on your deck with Juno and Sitka while I put clean sheets on your bed. Or, would you rather stay
with George and me? We have plenty of room."

"Thanks, you guys are wonderful and I love you. I think I would rather stay in the cottage."

"Okay, I want your doctor's information and I want you to keep our phone with you at all times so if you need us, we can be there quickly."

Vicki felt so loved and cared for. She sat in the sun with Juno on one side and Sitka on the other. It was like they knew.

Kathleen came out and told her the bedroom was ready. When she walked in there were flowers on her night stand and the bed was turned down. She started crying because she knew her husband would never do anything like this for her.

"There-there sweetheart. You know we love you like a daughter so let us take care of you. There is a reason we had this cottage on our property. We were waiting for someone to move in whom we could love and it's you, of course."

Vicki removed her makeup, took a quick shower, and went to bed. Immediately, she fell asleep knowing she was going to be fine and her child would be loved. Later, Kathleen came in with homemade chicken soup and tea. Vicki ate the soup, drank the tea and immediately felt better. However, because of the doctor's order, she had to stay in bed.

Okay, I'll work on the nonprofit foundation, she said to herself.

She placed a call to Ashley and left a message. She went back to sleep. Suddenly, she felt a wet nose and doggie kisses.

"Hey girls, I bet you are hungry. I'll feed you. Surely, I can do that much."

She went to the kitchen to get the dog food.

"You stay right where you are dear, I'll feed the girls." said George as he carried groceries into the kitchen.

She remembered Shirley had called as she thought to herself, I might as well get it over with. And, she went back to bed.

"Hi Shirley, it's Vicki."

"Hi Sweetie, what is going on?"

"I'm pregnant and Ted doesn't want the baby so I have moved to the cottage. My doctor put me on bed rest for a week."

"Does Ted know you're on bed rest?"

"No, of course not, he doesn't call. I did see him today and he said he needed to talk to me immediately."

"Let me talk to my son, I'll set him straight. He has always been a problem. What can I do for you? Is it ok if I come by?"

"Just be my friend. It's so sad because I think Ted would be a great dad. Come by anytime."

Shirley hung up and Vicki tried to go back to sleep when her phone rang and it was Ted.

"HEY, when I said I needed to talk to you, I MEANT IT! You are still my wife."

"What do you want Ted? I'm tired and my doctor has ordered bed rest for a week. I don't need nor want any type of added stress."

"I want you to come to your senses. We don't need a kid to mess up our life together. I don't want to share you with anyone."

"Well, I am going to have our baby. You will either be a dad or leave me. That's my stand and I'm not changing."

"We obviously don't have anything else to talk about. I will fight you over child support since I'm not even positive it is mine."

"How dare you! You are the one who hasn't been faithful. You bastard, when you can be civil, maybe then we can talk. And, if you're worried about the father of my child, I will gladly consent to a DNA test."

She slammed the phone down and cried.

Stop it. He's a jerk, you don't need to let him treat you like this, she told herself.

The next day she was restless and started planning her new life. Did she want to stay in Stone Mountain or did she want to go home to Colorado?

Ashley called and reported on her appointment with the attorney regarding the nonprofit foundation.

"This is so exciting. Thank you so much, now I can use my mind while I'm on bed rest."

"Bed rest? What is going on?"

"I'm pregnant and Ted is insisting I get rid of it and I'm not going to. So, we are living apart. My doctor put me on bed rest for a week. So, I have plenty of free time."

"I'm so sorry, Vicki. Ted will come around. These guys have such egos that creating another copy of themselves is something they should want to do. Jason was always a jerk, too."

"Well, I don't want a husband who won't help raise our child. So, I'm starting to plan my life without Ted."

"You know, I'll do anything to help. I'll forward the information from the foundation's attorney and let the wives know so we can get this thing off the ground. Talk to you soon. I love you." The phone rang again, it was Ted.

"Vicki, is it okay if I come by? Mom called and said you are on bed rest and I would like to bring dinner."

"Okay, I can't argue. If we can have a civil dinner, it will be fine."

"I'll be there in fifteen minutes."

Obviously, he was already on his way, thought Vicki. Just like him to be so sure of himself.

Ted arrived with food from Vicki's favorite seafood restaurant.

"I didn't know what you can and cannot eat, so I guessed. I brought you fresh trout and a salad. No wine."

"Thank you. It smells good and looks wonderful."

Ted found a bed tray and brought the food in for Vicki. He pulled a chair up to the bed for himself and they ate in silence for several minutes. Finally, Ted broke the silence. Vicki listened and tried to remain calm.

"Vicki, we just don't need a baby right now. I am traveling so much and I want you to be able to go with me."

"We can afford a nanny and I could travel with you. Plus, I know your parents would love to take care of our child when we are away."

"I just can't do it Vicki. Even though I care for you, this is not the life I want for myself. I want to be fair to you so we will discuss finances. Figure out how much you need a month to live a comfortable life. I assume you will work, so please be fair."

With that Ted took the dishes to the kitchen, put them in the sink and, without saying another word, left. Kathleen came in to see if Vicki was okay, then went to the kitchen to wash the dishes. She returned to the bedroom and sat on the bed holding Vicki's hand.

"I don't know what to do. Should I stay here or move?" Vicki asked.

"Vicki, right now you don't need to make any big decisions. We are here for you."

The next day Vicki started planning her new life. She felt guilty that she was excited.

"Okay girls and baby, what are we going to do with our lives?"

# 12

## A New Life

As the months went by, Vicki started to settle into her new life as a pregnant, single woman, and the founder and CEO of a nonprofit foundation.

After many conference calls, the wives decided to name the nonprofit foundation "The Caring Wives Foundation." Instead of just helping families of asbestos victims, they decided to help families of victims injured by any harmful products.

At first, only the five asbestos wives were involved. Then, as word got out, other attorneys' wives contacted them about helping. Vicki was so proud and pleased with the progress of the Foundation.

As time went by, the Foundation received more and more funding. Soon, the wives were ready to start disbursing the money. All of them waived any salary, opting instead to put all finances into the Foundation.

At one of the meetings of the wives, it was decided that the Foundation headquarters would be in Boulder, Colorado. Vicki was planning on moving to Boulder, where she had always felt at home.

The next order of business was to find the best way to help the families of products liability victims. They all agreed that it would be ideal to have a place where the families, and especially the children, could get away from the problems of everyday life. The acquisition of land would have to wait.

One morning as Vicki was packing for the move, she felt a sharp pain, worse than anything she had ever felt before. She yelled out and the dogs immediately came to her side and started howling. Kathleen heard Juno and Sitka and came running to the cottage where she found Vicki unconscious. She immediately called 911, Vicki's doctor, Barb, and Shirley.

When Vicki woke up in a hospital room, she immediately knew something was wrong. Shirley was sitting beside her holding her hand.

"What happened?" asked Vicki.

"Honey, I am so sorry; you had a miscarriage."
replied Shirley.

Vicki felt like her world had just ended and couldn't stop the tears. Doctor Carter came in and told her the baby would never have survived and there was nothing Vicki could have done to save the baby. As Dr. Carter left the room, he told the nurse to give Vicki a sedative and watch her to make sure she was sleeping.

When Vicki woke up, Ted was sitting beside her bed, holding her hand. He looks awful, Vicki thought.

"Vicki, I'm so sorry. Even though I didn't want this child, I know you did."

"Ted, just go away, I don't want to see you."

Later that day, Barb came by and told Vicki that all the packing was finished for the move.

"Oh, Barb, you didn't have to do that. I don't know when I'll be able to leave."

"Well, it's done and I am taking time off to drive to Boulder with you."

"Thank you so much. I am going to miss you. I did hear from the realtor before the miscarriage and she found a cottage for me to rent. It sounds delightful and has three bedrooms, so there is plenty of room for you." Vicki told Barb.

Later that day Dr. Carter checked on her and said she could go home the next day and would be well enough to leave for Colorado in three days. He had contacted a doctor in Boulder who would take her as a patient.

Vicki slept well that night and had a dream about a little girl with long curls. The girl smiled at Vicki and said she was anxious to meet her.

The next morning Barb took her back to the cottage. Vicki was glad to see the dogs and they howled their welcomes and stayed by her side. The cottage was filled with flowers, mostly from Ted. On the table, Vicki saw an envelope addressed to her in Ted's handwriting. Inside was a check made payable to the Foundation in the amount of $500,000.

"Well, guess he is feeling guilty." Barb said.

"Don't care what made him do this, I'll take it, we need money for the Foundation."

Barb spent the night at the cottage. The next morning, Vicki was feeling better and anxious to get moving.

"Barb, let's leave this afternoon. I feel better and really

want to get out of here."

"Okay, I'm ready. Luckily, my judge is on vacation so I can be gone as long as you need me. He gave me his blessing, so off we go!"

Vicki called the movers and told them how to get into the cottage, called her realtor in Boulder to say they would be in Boulder in two days, and sent the wives an email suggesting a meeting of the Foundation Board in a week.

She and Barb went by the bank to deposit the Foundation check into five separate accounts for the Foundation. They went back to the cottage to get the dogs and say goodbye to the Martins.

"I feel like I'm leaving my family." cried Vicki.

"We do too, dear."

"The movers are coming tomorrow to get my stuff and I have arranged for the cottage to be cleaned the day after so you can rent it again."

"Vicki, we are not going to rent the cottage, it is here for you anytime you want it. Ted came by and we agreed on a reduced rent, although we didn't want to take any money, he insisted. It is for your use only; he will not be staying there."

At first, Vicki felt angry then decided to let Ted do something nice for her.

As Vicki and Barb pulled out of the driveway, an auto transport pulled in to take Vicki's Z4 to Boulder. George waved Vicki on, saying he would take care of it.

As Vicki drove away from Stone Mountain, she had mixed emotions. She felt a great sense of relief to be away from Ted and all those problems. Also, she felt sad because she loved Stone Mountain.

## 13

## *Boulder*

After two days on the road, Vicki, Barb and the dogs arrived in Boulder, Colorado. Vicki immediately felt like she was home and was excited to start her totally new life here.

They went to the realtor's office to pick up the key for the cottage. The cottage was located up Boulder Canyon and had two acres of land for her dogs to run and explore.

When they opened the door to the cottage, Vicki stopped and smiled. It was open and light. The cottage was large enough for an office and had enough room for the wives to stay when they held board meetings. The kitchen was totally modern and user friendly.

"Barb, other than the cottage in Stone Mountain, this is my home." said Vicki.

"Wow, wish I could stay here with you." exclaimed Barb.

"Are you serious? The Foundation is going to need an administrator."

"Really, I would love the job."

"Tomorrow, we'll talk to the Board, set up a meeting and first on the agenda will be hiring you and deciding on your salary." That night, after a day of unpacking, Vicki slept soundly. The little girl with the curls appeared again.

The following morning there was a knock on the door and the four other wives walked in with flowers, wine and many binders.

"What a surprise!" exclaimed Vicki. "I was going to call and suggest a board meeting."

"Well, we're here, we have rented an Airbnb and are ready to go to work." said Ashley.

"Ladies, meet Barb, my bestie from Stone Mountain. She would love to be our administrator."

"Hello Barb," they said in unison.

After coffee, juice and English muffins, the ladies sat at the round kitchen table and got to work. After a full day of working, they passed resolutions, hired Barb for more than she was earning in Stone Mountain, approved a newspaper article, approved the minutes of the organization meeting, and started making plans for their first family to be supported by the Foundation.

After the work was done, they went to the Red Lion for dinner. They ate and drank wine, laughed and felt so good about what they were doing. As promised, none of the meals, travel and lodging, were charged to the Foundation. All the money in the Foundation bank accounts, including the $500,000 Ted left for Vicki, was for the charitable work of the Foundation and Barb's salary, benefits and taxes.

Vicki was loving her new life, even though at times a

sadness crept over her when she thought about her baby. To make up for it, she threw herself into the work of the Foundation. The curly headed girl made appearances often in her dreams.

Barb had moved to Boulder and the wives talked on a daily basis. The Foundation had a list of needy families and it felt good to be able to help them with medical bills, housing and everyday needs. Vicki still wanted someplace special where the families could go to get away from their problems. That will have to wait thought Vicki.

One day, out of the blue, Vicki answered her phone and Ted was on the other end of the line.

"Hello Vicki, it's Ted."

"Ted, you sound terrible, are you okay?"

"No, I'm not. It seems I have contracted asbestosis. Isn't that ironic?"

"Oh Ted, I am so sorry... how?" cried Vicki, tears filling her eyes.

"When I worked in the mines in high school. Guess it serves me right."

"No, you don't deserve this. What can I do?"

"Could you come to Stone Mountain? I have some things to talk to you about."

"Of course, when do you want me to come?"

"As soon as possible, I am pretty bad and who knows how long I have."

"Oh, Ted, I will be there tomorrow."

After she hung up, she walked into the office and told Barb what was going on.

"Can you stay here and take care of the girls? I don't

know why you don't move out of that hovel you are living in and stay here permanently."

"Of course, I'll stay. We'll talk about the rest of it when you get back."

The next morning Vicki went to the airport to buy a ticket and go to Montana. As she walked into the terminal at DIA, there was a page for her. She went to a courtesy phone and standing beside it was Ben.

"Ben, what are you doing here?"

"Ted's firm sent the plane to get you so we need to go to the private terminal."

Once, they were airborne, Vicki asked Ben, "How bad is he?"

"Bad, probably a week."

The rest of the flight Vicki sat in shocked silence trying to imagine Ted not being in control of everything around him. All of a sudden, she realized they were not officially divorced. She was still his wife.

## 14

## *Goodbye*

When they landed, a limo was waiting for her. Ted's parents were in the back. Vicki hugged them both, and the tears started. She couldn't stop crying.

Henry spoke first, "We don't want you to be shocked when you see Ted. He's going to die soon, and he wants to get his affairs in order."

Shirley was holding Vicki's hand and said, "He really loves you, dear, and deeply regrets how he acted."

When they reached the hospital, and as Vicki walked into Ted's private room, she caught her breath. Lying in the bed was a person who no longer resembled Ted. He was sleeping. When he sensed her presence, he opened his eyes and smiled.

"Hello, beautiful."

"Oh, Ted, I am so sorry. What can I do?"

"Just be with me. There are many things I want to talk to you about. Why don't you get settled, and then we'll start? Ben knows what I want, so he will be here too."

"Vicki, dear, we want you to stay with us through this." said Henry. "After all, we are still family."

"Thank you, Henry, I would love to be with you through this."

After Henry and Shirey left, Vicki sat by Ted's bed, holding his hand.

"First," Ted said, "I want to apologize to you. You were the best thing to happen to me and I threw it away because of my inflated ego and fear of loving someone."

"Ted, let's not dwell on the past."

"Vicki, I need to get this out before it is too late. I love you to the point it scares me. I felt myself losing control of my life because I was too selfish to share it with anyone. When you lost the baby, I wanted to scream. I would have loved to have a little girl with curls running around the island with the dogs."

Vicki actually jumped when Ted mentioned the girl with curls.

What does that mean? she thought.

After talking about their life and regrets, Ted was very tired, and getting quite weak. Vicki said she would return the next morning.

"Tell Ben he needs to be here, too."

Ben took Vicki to the Winters' mansion. For the first time, Vicki felt like she belonged there.

As they ate dinner, they all talked about Ted and what he meant to them. By the end of the dinner, there was laughter in addition to tears.

"Ted would have wanted this," said Vicki.

She slept that night, dreaming about a little girl with curls.

The next morning, Vicki and Ben went back to the hospital. Ted looked even weaker than he did the night before and he was having difficulty breathing. The doctor had put him on oxygen.

Vicki went to the bed, kissed Ted on his pale forehead, sat down and held his hand.

"Are you ready, Ben?" asked Ted.

"Yes, I have everything right here."

"Vicki, I have appointed Ben as the executor and administrator of my estate. I have asked Ben to summarize my last wishes and read them to you now. I don't want you to say anything until he has finished. I know you never knew how much money I had because I was afraid to tell you; why I don't know. Isn't it silly how when you are at the end of your life, you are no longer afraid?

With that, Ben read from the statement previously dictated by Ted.

"*First*, as you are aware, the petition for dissolution of our marriage has not been filed. So, it will be easier for Ben to settle my estate.

*Second*, all of my liquid assets are yours. All I ask is that you maintain a lifestyle you want, and if you want, use the money for your Foundation. The total amount of liquid assets is approximately twenty million dollars.

*Third*, all cars, boats and personal items are yours to do with as you wish.

*Fourth*, we come to the island and the buildings. After you left, I had a lodge built on the island. I would like it if you would use the lodge and the island for your Foundation. I remember you saying you would love to have a place for the families to get away from their daily problems."

"Oh, Ted," said Vicki, tears running down her cheeks. "You are way too generous. I would love to use the island for the Foundation. I will make sure the island is named after you."

Speaking in almost a whisper, Ted said, "Vicki, this morning the doctor said I will have to go on life support and I don't want that. I have an DNR and you are my agent. I'm asking that I not be put on life support. Just let me die. There is no getting out of this alive."

"Ted," Vicki said through her tears, "I will do whatever you want. Just know that I love you and always will."

She leaned over and kissed him on his parched lips. At that moment, the doctor came in.

"I'm ready, doc, as soon as my parents come in." gasped Ted.

Henry and Shirley walked in.
"I will leave you alone with Ted." said Ben, wiping his eyes.

"No, Ben, I want you here." coughed Ted.

So, with Henry and Shirley on one side of the bed, Ben standing at the foot and Vicki sitting on the other side of the bed, holding Ted's hand, the doctor gave Ted a shot and let him drift off to sleep. Later that night, Vicki and Ted were alone. He opened his eyes, smiled at her and in a soft voice that cracked, as he whispered,

"I love you and our girl with the curls."

Vicki broke down crying, then realized Ted had squeezed her hand, let go, and was no longer breathing.

It was over.

# 15

## Life After Ted

The day after Ted passed away, Vicki, Henry and Shirley made arrangements to have him cremated.

"Henry and Shirley, would it be okay to bury some of Ted's ashes on the island? I have decided to name the island "The Ted Winter Memorial Island".

"Honey, he would be so honored. Also, Henry and I would love to help with the work on the island when you bring the families here. As you know, we have our own King Air plane that we hardly ever use. We will donate it's use to bring families here. It is a ten-passenger plane." said Shirley.

"Oh, I am so fortunate to have you in my life."

After a brief, private ceremony on the island, Vicki knew she had to decide where she wanted to live, on the island or in Boulder. Finally, she decided to move back to Stone Mountain, live on the island and, if the Martin's agreed, let Barb have the cottage. Barb brought the dogs back to the island.

The next week, the wives came and were so excited to

have the first families come for a week of pampering and fun. Staff was hired and after a month of preparation, the Foundation was ready to hold a grand opening for all donors and workers.

Accommodations were arranged, including using the cottage, Henry and Shirley's mansion and the island. As the donors and others arrived at the dock, they were greeted with a sign on the gate to the property that said: "The Ted Winter Memorial Island".

After a two-day grand opening, the donors and others left. The Board met and decided on the first two families to be guests. Since it was spring, the island was beautiful with wildflowers and wildlife.

Vicki helped get everything ready for the first visitors. There were two families with parents and two children each. Vicki had purchased some horses, ponies, goats, rabbits, dogs, cats and other animals for the visitors to enjoy.

She heard the boat arriving at the dock and walked down to meet the first guests. Ashley, Sherry, Frankie and Stephanie were all there with Vicki.

First to get off the boat was a family who looked around in awe. It was obvious the husband ,and father was ill, even though, his eyes shined as he watched his two children run down the dock to greet Juno and Sitka. The huskies played their role perfectly.

The second family disembarked and had the same reaction. This time Juno, Sitka and the two other children came running back to claim the two new boys. Off they went to run and play. The staff in charge of children, immediately took the kids under their wings.

"Please come and get settled in your accommodations." said Ashley.

The parents started walking up the dock. For some reason Vicki stayed behind, smiling because she felt her life was right where it was supposed to be.

"Hello?" a small voice said from behind her.

Vicki turned and looked into the bluest eyes she had ever seen. Standing before her was a beautiful girl who was about ten-years old with curls hanging down her back.

After Vicki recovered from the shock of seeing her dream standing in front of her, she said,

"Hello, what can I do for you?"

"Both of my parents died from asbestosis and I wanted a place to recover and decide what to do with my life. I have no other family."

"You do now, what is your name?"

"Donna."

"Well, Donna, let's get your things into the main house, you are home my dear."

## Acknowledgments

I want to thank my husband, Ben Echeverria, for seven years of patience during which I was writing this book and for his help in publishing my first novel. I also want to thank my wonderful friends, Anna, Candy, and Stephanie. They have taught me the true meaning of friendship.

# End Notes

[1] From Wikipedia the following information introduces the subject of asbestos and related information.(See: (https://en.wikipedia.org/wiki/Asbestos )

"**Asbestos** (pronounced /æsˈbɛstəs/ or /æzˈbɛstəs/) is a set of six naturally occurring silicate minerals,[1] which all have in common their eponymous asbestiform habit: long (roughly 1:20 aspect ratio), thin fibrous crystals, with each visible fiber composed of millions of microscopic "fibrils" that can be released by abrasion and other processes.[2] They are commonly known by their colors, as "blue asbestos", "brown asbestos", "white asbestos", and green asbestos.

Asbestos mining existed more than 4,000 years ago, and large-scale mining began at the end of the 19th century, when manufacturers and builders began using asbestos because of its desirable physical properties:[1] sound absorption, average tensile strength, its resistance to fire, heat, electrical and chemical damage, and affordability. It was used in such applications as electrical insulation for hotplate wiring and in building insulation. When asbestos is used for its resistance to fire or heat, the fibers are often mixed with cement or woven into fabric or mats. These desirable properties made asbestos a very widely used material, and its use continued to grow throughout most of the 20th century until the carcinogenic effects of asbestos dust caused its effective demise as a mainstream construction and fireproofing material in most countries.

It is now known that prolonged inhalation of asbestos fibers can cause serious and fatal illnesses including malignant lung cancer, mesothelioma, and asbestosis (a type of pneumoconiosis).[3][4] Health issues related to asbestos exposure can be found in records dating back to Roman times. By the beginning of the 20th century concerns were beginning to be raised, which escalated in severity during the 1920s and 1930s. By the 1980s and 1990s asbestos trade and use started to become banned outright, phased out, or heavily restricted in an increasing number of countries.

The severity of asbestos-related diseases, the material's extremely widespread use in many areas of life, its continuing long-term use after harmful health effects were known or suspected, and fact that asbestos-related diseases can emerge decades after exposure ceases, have resulted in asbestos litigation becoming the longest, most expensive mass tort in U.S. history and a much lesser legal issue in most other countries involved, being handled much more responsibly.[5] Asbestos-related liability also remains an ongoing concern for many manufacturers, insurers and reinsurers.

www.ingramcontent.com/pod-product-compliance
Lightning Source LLC
Chambersburg PA
CBHW022029170626
46808CB00003B/1114